Library of
Davidson College

HAYDN'S *STURM UND DRANG* SYMPHONIES

Form and Meaning

William E. Grim

Studies in the History and Interpretation of Music
Volume 23

The Edwin Mellen Press
Lewiston/Queenston/Lampeter

Library of Congress Cataloging-in-Publication Data

Grim, William E.
  Haydn's "Sturm und Drang" symphonies : form and meaning / William E. Grim.
     p.   cm. -- (Studies in the history and interpretation of music ; v. 23)
  Includes bibliographical references.
  ISBN 0-88946-448-0
  1. Haydn, Joseph, 1732-1809. Symphonies. 2. Symphony.
I. Title. II. Title: "Sturm und Drang" symphonies. III. Series
ML410.H4G73 1990
784.2'184'092--dc20   89-13328
                                                                       CIP
                                                                       MN

This is volume 23 in the continuing series
Studies in the History & Interpretation of Music
Volume 23 ISBN 0-88946-448-0
SHIM Series ISBN 0-88946-426-X

A CIP catalog record for this book
is available from the British Library.

Copyright © 1990 William E. Grim

All rights reserved. For information contact

The Edwin Mellen Press   The Edwin Mellen Press
Box 450   Box 67
Lewiston, New York   Queenston, Ontario
USA 14092   CANADA L0S 1L0

The Edwin Mellen Press, Ltd.
Lampeter, Dyfed, Wales
UNITED KINGDOM SA48 7DY

Printed in the United States of America

For Debby

TABLE OF CONTENTS

Chapter		Page
I.	Origins of the <u>Sturm und Drang</u> Controversy	1
II.	Form	37
III.	Process	69
IV.	Morphology	121
V.	Conclusions	149
	Bibliography	155
	Index	159

PREFACE

Words are the raw material of scholarship. Used properly, one word may impart generations of accumulated knowledge within a fraction of a second. On the other hand, the improper use of words may confuse an area of intellectual endeavor for years to come. Nowhere is this problem more acute than in the discipline of musicology, whose subject matter by definition is not easily given over to literary description and analysis. Musicologists themselves are only too aware of this situation. Jack Westrup has reminded us that:

> The function of words is to impart information, to sustain argument, and to excite emotion. Too often, however, they are used as a substitute for thinking.[1]

Although the above quotation was concerned with humanistic writing as a whole, it could have been written specifically about the scholarship concerning the question of whether or not a musical _Sturm und Drang_ style exists. Probably in no other area of musicology has there been such a pronounced discrepancy as there exists between the music of the so-called _Sturm und Drang_ and the words used to describe it by a wide variety of scholars.

The challenge before the author, therefore, is to change the intellectual climate from the condition whereby _a priori_ ideas determine the analysis of the music purportedly contained in this category, to that in which the empirical data of musical analysis determines the description of the music and whether or not these works constitute a separate and distinguishable style category.

---

[1] Jack A. Westrup, "The Paradox of Eighteenth-Century Music," in _Studies in Musicology_, ed. James Pruett (Chapel Hill: University of North Carolina Press, 1969), p. 118.

and whether or not these works constitute a separate and distinguishable style category.

The overall plan of investigation in this book will be to take the Sturm und Drang symphonies of Haydn (Nos. 39 [ca. 1766-67], 35 [1767], 59 [ca. 1767], 38 [ca. 1767], 49 [1768], 58 [ca. 1768], 26 [1768-69], 41 [ca. 1768-69], 48 [ca. 1768-69], 44 [ca. 1770-71], 52 [ca. 1770-71], 43 [ca. 1770-71], 42 [1771], 51 [ca. 1771-73], 45 [1772], 46 [1772], 47 [1772], and 65 [ca. 1772-73]) and compare them to representative examples of the rest of his symphonic output, and to try to determine whether these works are of a style sui generis, or whether they show traces of being part of a lifelong stylistic development of symphonic writing. Most of the literature concerning the Sturm und Drang works attempts to explain away their unique nature by invoking a societal or sociological explanation. Generally this assumes the form of an author explaining about the isolation of Haydn at the Estherházy estate, the newfound artistic "freedom" that Haydn felt around 1767 when he assumed the duties of head kapellmeister, and a succeeding period of retrenchment after his realization that he had gone too far with his musical experimentation.

This approach seems somewhat dubious for two reasons. First of all, the aforementioned explanation of the Sturm und Drang works is the result of examining only the influence of external pressures upon Haydn. The music itself is considered in a tangential manner, if at all. External factors may have a great deal to do with precipitating the composition of a work of music, but may have absolutely nothing to do with the musical ideas contained in that work. In addition, it is very well documented that the influence of Fux's contrapuntal ideas was strongly felt by Haydn throughout his artistic career. One of the hallmarks of Fuxian musical pedagogy is that ideas should be systematically and thoroughly exploited. In looking at Haydn's oeuvre, one can see that forms were not always used in their mature states immediately but were revised and adapted throughout the course of many years. Therefore, the second reason for doubting the "sudden" and "unrelated" labeling of the Sturm und Drang symphonies of Haydn is that it seems illogical that a composer, whose technical and formal ideas were so consistently and thoroughly pursued within a neo-Fuxian tradition, would arrive at new principles of formal and stylistic synthesis without noticeable examples of intermediate stages of development. For Haydn to have arrived at a new compositional style labeled Sturm und Drang and then to peremptorily abandon it appears to be out of his character as a creative artist.

For the purposes of this book, the Sturm und Drang symphonies will be compared to two distinct groups of symphonies:

(1) Fürnberg-Morzin symphonies (ca. 1757-1761): Nos. 1, 37, 18, 2, 15, 4, 10, 32, 5, 11, 33, 27, 107, 3

(2) London symphonies (1791-1795): Nos. 93-104

Readers of this book are advised to consult the Critical Edition of the Complete Symphonies of Joseph Haydn edited by H. C. Robbins Landon for the musical passages mentioned in parentheses in the text. As a convention, musical examples are given in the text only in cases where it is deemed absolutely essential. The wide circulation of the Landon edition makes it unnecessary to list all of the multitude of musical examples (many of which are known to most of the potential readership of this volume) which are referred to in the body of this study.

Finally, the author would be remiss if he did not mention all of the people who provided advice or gave support in the process of completing this study: Professor Herbert Horn, Mrs. Olga Horn, Professor Aubrey Garlington, Professor Eleanor McCrickard, Professor Harold Schwartz, Professor Ernest Harriss, and Professor David A. Sheldon. The author would like to thank in particular Professor Herbert Richardson of the Edwin Mellen Press whose interest in and support of this project and others have been of such significance in the author's career. The greatest debt of all, however, is owed to the author's wife Deborah, without whose support this work would never have been brought to its fruition either in its original state as the author's dissertation or in this present revision.

It is the sincere wish of the author that his reasoning will not be judged too eristic and that any original ideas or interpretations (however modest) will not be seen as conclusions, but as the stimuli for further questioning. Finally, any remaining errors, factual or critical, contained in this study are the sole responsibility of the author.

William E. Grim
Athens, Ohio
August 1989

CHAPTER I

ORIGINS OF THE STURM UND DRANG CONTROVERSY

> See what things are in themselves, dividing them into matter, form and purpose.
> -----Marcus Aurelius, Meditations
> XII: 10

Historiography

The perception of a work of music as an historical and/or aesthetic document is influenced by several factors. One, any work of art is viewed within the context of its time of creation as indicative of, or opposed to, what is considered to be the prevailing stylistic tendencies of that era. Two, unlike the "events" of general history, a work of art is a living aesthetic artifact or object whose influence may extend not just to immediately succeeding works but, in varying degrees, to the future as well. In other words, a work of art is constantly being reinterpreted and rediscovered, with its aesthetic value, historical context, and formal structures subject to what may be termed as the mutability of history. This history of the interpretation and analysis of artworks (Wirkungsgeschichte) is precisely that with which this study is concerned.

Both methods of critical perception appear in varying degrees in all fine arts scholarship, even if only at the subconscious level. It is impossible to consider a work of art in terms of rigorously scientific style criticism without being influenced by such subjective criteria as the interpretations and value judgments of the generations subsequent to the creation of the work of art itself. However, since positivism so pervades the field of musicology, scientific style criticism has become (and remains to a great degree) the paradigm of music scholarship. This method is extremely well suited for the works of the various Kleinmeisters and for such categories as folk music and Tafelmusik because of their susceptibility to generalizations and statistical analysis. Canonized musical compositions, however, rarely lend themselves to style criticism because such works tend to be unusual rather than typical in construction. Often, scholars who are attempting to deal with canonized compositions find that in order to provide a framework of understanding they must leave the narrow confines of style criticism and appropriate the methodologies of philosophy, sociology, intellectual history, and comparative literature. In so doing, these scholars knowingly or unwittingly contribute to the expansion of the Wirkungsgeschichte of the works they are attempting to comprehend and define. Over the course of several generations, then, this "created history" can take on the aura of conventional wisdom or even statistical data.

It is just such a situation that exists in the scholarship concerning the Sturm und Drang symphonies of Joseph Haydn. As will be demonstrated later in this chapter, when musicologists first became interested in what came to be known as the Sturm und Drang period, it was apparent to them that they did not possess an outline of a musical origin by which to judge these seemingly unusual compositions. Logically, they sought recourse in the most extraordinary non-musical artistic phenomenon of the same time period, namely, the German literary Sturm und Drang which was thought to be representative of the Zeitgeist of the period of 1770 to 1780. In recent decades, however, there has been a vast expansion of factual knowledge of eighteenth-century music which is in need of being synthesized and examined in relation to accepted scholarly assumptions. The task of this author, therefore, is twofold: (1) to determine the degree to which our knowledge of what is now known as the musical Sturm und Drang (in particular, the Sturm und Drang symphonies of Joseph Haydn) is based upon "created history," and (2) having done so, to attempt to reconstruct the history of these compositions in terms more closely related to the nature of music itself. This bifurcation of purpose is essential for a new understanding of the compositions to come into being. It is not enough to point out the flaws of previous scholarship if they exist; ideally one should offer a reasonable and compelling alternative, for as Carl Dahlhaus states in Foundations of Music History:

> At the moment the advocates of a sociological approach to the historiography of music are still largely basking in their unfair advantage of being able to criticize the deficiencies of traditional music history instead of having to justify their own results, which are far too few. But, of course, the triumphs of programmatic historians over their more practically minded colleagues have seldom been lasting.[1]

Elaboration of Terminology

For the purposes of this study it is necessary to elaborate further upon the following musical terms.

(1) Form. The traditionally accepted description of the Sturm und Drang symphonies of Haydn generally contains words to the effect that

---

[1]Carl Dahlhaus, Foundations of Music History, trans. J. B. Robinson (New York: Cambridge University Press, 1983), p. 10

Haydn departed from "traditional formal patterns." Usually, no support is given to this statement. It remains to be examined whether or not the Sturm und Drang symphonies are essentially of a different formal design from the rest of Haydn's symphonies. There is the probability that seemingly developed "styles" may be, in fact, intermediate stages in the overall growth of a composer's stylistic development. Although formal procedures are subject to growth and expansion, there is the additional possibility that what may appear on the surface to be a dramatic departure from "traditional formal patterns" may be a stylistic change with overall formal patterns remaining relatively constant.

(2) Process. The compositional procedures that composers utilize in their works reveal a great deal about the rational (and rhetorical) basis of their compositions. Stylized procedures may be looked upon as harbingers of specific types of further musical development. This is a particularly fruitful area of exploration and one that has received very little application in the analysis of music. Janet M. Levy has suggested three compositional processes that serve as syntactical agents: (1) broken bass patterns such as the Alberti bass; (2) solos; and (3) unison passages.[2] The late Arnold Salop suggested the possibility that the presentation of musical tautologies takes place an overwhelmingly large percentage of the time during periods of low harmonic and rhythmic intensity.[3] Another possibility is that of the syntactical shift

---

[2]Janet M. Levy, "Texture as a Sign in Classic Music," Journal of the American Musicological Society 35 (1982): 482-531.

[3]Arnold Salop, "Intensity in the Classical Sonata-Allegro," in Studies in the History of Musical Style (Detroit: Wayne State University Press, 1971), pp. 215-250.

from homophonic to contrapuntal texture and vice versa. The examination of compositional processes, therefore, offers an almost unlimited field of inquiry. If the _Sturm und Drang_ symphonies are as unique as many scholars suggest, it would be logical to assume that the processes involved in their composition would reveal differences in compositional procedure from preceding and succeeding symphonies.

(3) _Morphology_. The study of morphology, i.e., the articulation (or presentation), derivation, and combination of structural units without regard specifically to their functions or contexts, is a relatively new area of music analysis. Leonard Meyer has suggested that the fulfillment of implied tonal goals is so strong an urge with Mozart that even when he disrupts a compositional procedure (Meyer lists four such procedures: (1) circle of fifths; (2) other sequence patterns; (3) fourth species counterpoint; and (4) a combination of the above) the music reaches the tonal goal that it would have reached if the procedure had not been disrupted in the first place.[4] Utilizing these analytical procedures for Haydn's orchestral output should provide especially useful information and an excellent means to help determine whether or not the _Sturm und Drang_ symphonies constitute a radical departure from the norm of Haydn's symphonic writing. The importance of morphological study (beyond that of form and process) is that such an examination should help to reveal the composer's harmonic intentions at a level that is almost subconscious in its unfolding.

---

[4]Leonard Meyer, "Process and Morphology in the Music of Mozart," _The Journal of Musicology_ 1 (1982): 67-94.

The Coining of the Term "Sturm und Drang" and Its Use in Music Historiography

The use of the term <u>Sturm und Drang</u> to denote a period or sub-period of music history is the result of a curious origin and propagation the study of which reveals almost as many insights into the vagaries of certain methodologies of music historiography as it does to the specific musical works within its purview. The appropriation of this term from the literary world to that of the musical is a relatively recent phenomenon and stems directly from an article written by Theodore de Wyzewa entitled "A Propos du centenaire de la mort de Joseph Haydn" in the May-June 1909 edition of <u>Revue des deux mondes</u>. In this rather rambling retrospective overview of Haydn's career, Wyzewa writes a great deal about the unique qualities of the minor-keyed symphonies,[5] and then proffers the theory that they are the result of "romantic inspiration" which undoubtedly had its origin in some sort of a personal crisis:

> Evidently around 1772, there was an extremely acute "crisis" in the musical career of the master which was, moreover, as short-lived as it was unexpected and sudden: for not only do the works of 1773 retain no trace of the "romantic" inspiration of the preceding year, but, from this time onward, Joseph Haydn seems to employ his genius in the service of the new "galant" style of music, that will make of him for a long time the most learned and charming of the "entertainers." However, we would like to know under what influence this tragic--and providential--crisis arose which generated some of his most

---

[5]Theodore de Wyzewa, "A Propos du centenaire de la mort de Joseph Haydn," <u>Revue des deux mondes</u> 51 (May-June 1909): 939-943.

original compositions: but alas! his biography up to now is completely incapable of providing any information. To the contrary, for the year 1772, it speaks only of brilliant and joyous festivals in which Haydn and his companions took part: a reception at Eisenstadt for the Prince of Rohan, performances and concerts organized at Pressburg in honor of the Empress Maria Theresa. No event in the private life of the master signals either his endurance of his wife's ill-humor or even when he went so far as to write little church motets, knowing how much his eternal well-being meant to her and also to the satisfaction of his confessor. As for the singer Luigia Polzelli, the friend whose later love consoled the troubles of his home life, it will be seven years (1779) until he will meet her.

However, the documents are silent concerning the causes of this romantic "attack" of the composer of the Farewell and Passion [symphonies]. Rather, they do not tell us anything for certain: but one of them allows us to affirm the true existence, such as we guessed according to its effects, of such a crisis in the life of Haydn. A Viennese tradition of the first years of the past century has it that one of the three pathetic symphonies of 1772, Passion, was inspired by "his grief on the death of a beloved person." And we might be certain by this account that likewise arising from the same source is the plaintive Sonata in C Minor and the _Trauer_ Symphony which the old Haydn selected from among all his works to be performed at his burial. Yes, all of this music of grief was on account of the death of an extremely dear person: a young girl, very certainly, whom the Esterhaza kapellmeister had known, perhaps among the performing personnel of the estate--just as later on he would come to know Luigia Polzelli--and about whom he had faithfully borne his grief to the bottom of his old heart until the day when he was to settle his last will. I thought for a moment that this represents the inspiration of Haydn's romantic masterpieces in the form of an adorable child, Mlle Delphin, about whom the account informs us of having died of pulmonary congestion on June 18, 1772, the victim of too much ardor in dancing during the festival organized in honor of the Prince of Rohan; but Haydn's grief seems to go back to an earlier date, and without doubt, the world did not know the name of the "immortal beloved" whom he cherished.

Concerning which it is appropriate to add that if the source of the pathetic works of Haydn can have come to him only from personal emotions, the form which he gave to the aforementioned is the consequence of another great intellectual and moral crisis, which was at that time in the process of transforming the German arts. Several years before, Germany began to be obsessed with a new artistic spirit, born out of the foreign influence of Rousseau and Ossian, but nowhere else was to express itself with as much lustre or truly "romantic" brilliance. The historians have usually referred to this period of inflamed and vibrant agitation by the name <u>Sturm und Drang</u> which began around 1770, having found its real incarnation in 1774 in the <u>Leonore</u> of Burger and the <u>Sorrows of Young Werther</u>. The inner revolution that symbolized these two works from the literary world could not fail also to search for expressions in the popular language of Germany which was its music; and, indeed, nothing is more curious than to see about this same time an absolute equivalent of <u>Sturm und Drang</u> manifesting itself suddenly in all German composers, from Joseph Haydn to Gluck and Mozart, and also in masters of the second rank such as Vanhall and the Dittersdorfs.

But the study of this short "romantic" vista, which was soon interrupted among German musicians by the progress of "galanterie," would cause me to digress too far....[6]

---

[6]Ibid., pp. 943-945.

Evidemment, il y a eu aux environs de 1772, dans la carrière musicale du maître, une "crise" d'une acuité extrême, et d'ailleurs aussi passagère qu'imprévue et soudaine: car non seulement les oeuvres de l'année 1773 ne conservent plus aucune trace de l'inspiration "romantique" de ces confidences passionées de l'année d'avant, mais c'est depuis que Joseph Haydn nous apparaît employant son génie au service de ce style nouveau de musique "galante" qui fera vraiment de lui, pendant une longue période, le plus savant et le plus charmant de tous les "amuseurs." Aussi aimerions-nous à savoir sous quelle influence a pu survenir en lui cette crise tragique,--et providentielle,--d'où sont sorties pour quelques-unes de ses compositions les plus originales: mais, hélas! sa biographie est, jusqu'à présent, tout à fait hors d'état de nous renseigner. Elle ne nous parle, au contraire, pour toute l'année 1772, que de fêtes brillantes et joyeuses où le jeune Haydn et ses compagnons ont eu à prendre part: réception, à Eisenstadt, du prince de Rohan, représentations et concerts organisés à Presbourg en l'honneur de l'impératrice Marie-Thérèse. Aucun événement à signaler, non plus, dans l'existence privée du maître, qui continue à supporter patiemment la mauvaise humeur de sa femme, et pousse même la complaisance pour elle jusqu'à écrire de petits motets d'église, sachant combien elle a toujours à coeur son salut éternel, ainsi que la satisfaction de son confesseur. Quant à la cantatrice Luigia Polzelli, l'amie qui, plus tard, le consolera des ennuis de sa vie de ménage, c'est seulement sept plus tard, en 1779, qu'il aura l'occasion de la rencontrer.

Ainsi les documents son muets sur les causes de cet "accès" romantique de l'auteur des Adieux et de la Passione. Ou plutôt ils n'ont à nous apprendre aucun fait certain: mais l'un d'eux nous permet d'affirmer l'existence réelle, dans la vie de Haydn, d'une crise telle que nous la devinions d'après ses effets. Une tradition viennoise, ayant cours dès les premières du siècle passé, atteste que l'une des trois symphonies pathétiques de 1772, la Passione, a été inspirée au jeune maître par "son chagrin de la mort d'une personne aimée." Et nous pouvons être sûrs, à ce compte, que c'est également de la même source qu'ont jailli et la plaintive sonate et ut mineur, et cette Symphonie Funèbre que le vieux Haydn allait choisir, entre toutes ses oeuvres, pour être exécutée à son enterrement. Oui, tous ces chants de douleur ont eu pour cause la mort d'une personne infiniment chère: d'une jeune femme, très certainement, que le maître de chapelle d'Esterhaz aura connue peut-être parmi le personnel dramatique du château,--comme il allait connaître, ensuite, Luigia Polzelli,--et dont il aura fidèlement porté le deuil, au fond de son vieux coeur, jusqu'au jour où il a eu à régler ses volontés suprêmes. J'ai même songé un moment, à me représenter cette inspiratrice des chefs-d'oeuvre romantiques de Haydn sous la figure d'une adorable enfant, Mlle Delphin, dont la chronique nous informe qu'elle est morte d'une congestion pulmonaire, le 18 juin 1772, victime de l'ardeur trop passionée, de sa danse durant les fêtes organisées en l'honneur du prince de Rohan; mais la douleur de Haydn paraît bien remonter à une date plus ancienne, et jamais, sans doute, le monde ne saura le nom de l'"immortelle bien-aimée" qui nous l'a value.

A quoi il convient d'ajouter que, si le fond de ces oeuvres pathétiques

It is interesting to note that although Wyzewa deals largely with the idea that Haydn's unhappy marital life (culminating in his later relationship with Luigia Polzelli) was the main source of inspiration of the Sturm und Drang works, almost in passing he says that if this is not the case then undoubtedly it is the result of the influence of the German literary Sturm und Drang. This was indeed a rather meager beginning to an intellectual debate that has produced copious amounts of scholarship, both positive and negative.

Although the writing in his article is highly subjective and tendentious, in all fairness to Wyzewa, it must be pointed out that around 1909, even with the publication of the Mandyczewski catalogue, the chronology of the Haydn symphonies was confused, and it was assumed that the minor-keyed

---

de Haydn ne peut lui être venu que de ses sentimens personnels, la forme qu'il a donnée à ceux-ci est la conséquence d'une autre grande crise, intellectuelle et morale, qui était alors en train de transformer tous les domaines de l'art allemand. Depuis plusieurs années déjà, l'Allemagne commençait à être travaillée d'un état d'esprit nouveau, né sous les influences étrangères de Rousseau et d'Ossian, mais qui nulle autre part ne devait s'exprimer, à cette date, avec autant de relief ni de véritable éclat "romantique." Les historiens ont contuine de désigner du nom de Sturm und Drang cette période d'agitation enflammée et vibrante qui, inaugurée aux alentours de 1770, allait trouver son incarnation parfaite, en 1774, dans la Lenore de Burger et dan les Souffrances du jeune Werther. La révolution intime que symbolisaient ces deux ouvrages dans l'ordre littéraire n'avait pu manquer de chercher à se traduire, également, dans cette langue populaire de l'Allemagne qu'était sa musique; et, en effet, rien n'est plus curieux que de voir, vers ce même temps, un équivalent absolu du Sturm und Drang se manifester, tout à coup, chez tous les compositeurs allemands, depuis Joseph Haydn jusqu'à Gluck et Mozart, en passant par des maîtres de second ordre, tels que les Vanhall et les Dittersdorf.

Mais l'étude de cette brève échappée "romantique," bientôt interrompue et retardée, chez les musiciens allemands, par les progrès de la "galanterie," m'entraînerait trop loin....

symphonies were written in approximately a two-year period, specifically the years 1771 and 1772. Although it is now known that these symphonies were written over a longer period of time (ca. 1768-1772), from Wyzewa's viewpoint there was a certain logic in assuming that there was more than mere coincidence in the proximity in time of the debuts of the Trauersymphonie of Haydn and Götz von Berlichingen of Goethe.

The point of departure for this study is that while the details of Wyzewa's theory have been shown to be erroneous, the overall analytical and historical approach of the same author remains, to a great extent, in virtually the same state as it did in 1909, specifically, that the so-called Sturm und Drang symphonies of Haydn are of a style sui generis--one might say the result of spontaneous generation and the victim of summary execution. H. C. Robbins Landon is very explicit in this account:

> The withdrawal from Sturm und Drang in Haydn is fully as dramatic and unexpected as its arrival: to paraphrase Erasmus, Nihil enim surduis aut impotentius mari commoto, & tamen ad Domini jussam repente versum est in summum tranquillitatem. [For surely, nothing is more obdurate and more passing than the raging sea; and yet, it was suddenly turned into absolute tranquility at the command of the Lord.][7]

As will be shown in the following section, Landon is not alone in his claims for the Sturm und Drang, extravagant though they might be. The position of Landon and those who agree with him constitute what is practically a traditional interpretation of the musical Sturm und Drang,

---

[7]H. C. Robbins Landon, Haydn: Chronicle and Works, 5 vols. (Bloomington: Indiana University Press, 1976-1980), 2: 278-279.

directly stemming from Wyzewa's article of 1909.

Methods and Problems

One of the most perplexing difficulties in developing a rationale for the present study is that, with the sole exception of the heightened presence of the minor mode, there exists no consensus among scholars as to what constitutes the musical characteristics of the Sturm und Drang. Musicologists who have dealt with the musical Sturm und Drang are divided into two groups: (1) those who define the Sturm und Drang in the most general and equivocal musical terminology; and (2) those who attempt to give a precise delineation of the musical features of these same works.

Included among the former category are such redoubtable figures as Paul Henry Lang, Charles Rosen, and Jens Peter Larsen.
Lang's writings on this subject are entirely concerned with the Sturm und Drang qua an event in European (specifically German) intellectual and cultural history. Lang, in his monumental Music in Western Civilization does not view the musical Sturm und Drang within an evolving musical style, but as representative of the Zeitgeist of the 1770s:

> The development section, the battlefield of thematic struggle, became the center of gravity of the symphony, and this section already showed all the attributes we assign to the thematic material to the exhaustion of its last particle, and the stirring up of that irresistible wave which carries in the recapitulation. Imbued with the

> spirit of the Sturm und Drang, composers were no longer satisfied with the content used by the style galant; they were searching for more profound ideas which they might enhance and render eloquent by an appropriate form. Here began the modern symphony.[8]

Concomitant with this desire for more profound musical ideas, Lang views the Sturm und Drang as a musical style in which the passions (or affections) are more easily aroused than in their predecessors:

> But the apostles of the Sturm und Drang fell victim to the many problems they evoked. The passions whipped up to a frenzy settled and became purified, rude reality was transfigured in the fire of ideals, and creative force and form-building willpower united in a common task.[9]

In the preceding two quotations, it becomes obvious that Lang perceives the musical Sturm und Drang as a dialectic process between the conflicting goals of profundity and passion. The synthesis of such a dialectic can only be chaos or irrationality. Lang goes on to state:

> Romanticism was not a sort of chaos like the Sturm und Drang, nor was it a demoralization of classicism as it is still often regarded....The centrifugal forces engendered by the irrational elements taken over from the Sturm und Drang, slumbering in the womb of classicism, came into their own in the romantic

---

[8]Paul Henry Lang, Music in Western Civilization (New York: W.W. Norton & Co., 1941), p. 611.

[9]Ibid., p. 619.

era.[10]

In examining Lang's magnum opus there is also the striking realization that he has been profoundly influenced by the Apollonian-Dionysian dichotomy as put forward by Nietzsche, with the galant representing the former and the Sturm und Drang the latter:

> The centuries-long battle for liberty and form, ideal and reality, German aspirations and the forces of antiquity, came to a standstill, the sentimental irrationalism of the Sturm und Drang emptied into the quiet world of the idea and the result was an aesthetic world picture, a Germandom reborn from the spirit of Greece, purified of its conflicts: a Germanized Hellas.[11]

The previous quotation is quite remarkable in its reference to the "sentimental irrationalism" of the Sturm und Drang. Even though Lang has not defined musical profundity, passion, or irrationality, he then proceeds to create the new category of "sentimental" irrationalism, thereby combining terminology of the Sturm und Drang with that of the equally ill-defined Empfindsamkeit.

Charles Rosen is equally unspecific in his treatment of the Sturm und Drang. Fortunately, Rosen does not view the German literary movement as the fons et origo of the musical style, but takes the latter as an historical given. The following quotation from The Classical Style concerning Haydn's Sturm und Drang period is significant in that it reveals not only the very general nature of the author's description of the musical style, but also offers

---

[10]Ibid., p. 739.

[11]Ibid., p. 620.

an explanation of stylistic development from the Sturm und Drang to the High Classic that is the result of a remarkably weak logical process:

> There is, however, a genuine progress in style between early and late Haydn: the younger Haydn is a great master of a style that only imperfectly realizes what the language of his time had to offer, the later is the creator of a style that is an almost perfect instrument for exploiting the resources of that language. (In all this, I am, I hope, begging the question of the extent to which changes in style themselves precipitate changes in the common language.) It is a delicate point, and an idle one, whether Haydn could have arrived at so richly complex and so controlled a style by continuing in the direction that may have seemed so finely promising in 1770. Hindsight is cruel to unrealized possibilities. Yet it is worth remarking that the greatest success of Haydn's early style, its fierce dramatic power, was inseparable there from a harsh simplicity, a refusal of complex control, and a willingness at times to break almost any rhythmic pattern for the sake of a single effect. It is difficult to see how a richer art could have arisen from this often brutal contrast between a coarse but urgent regularity and a dazzling eccentricity except by abandoning the very virtues which made the style of the early 1770's so compelling--which is, indeed, what Haydn did. It is, perhaps, a pity that with the attainment of a more disciplined style, some of the fierce energy that was so admirable had gone out of his art. His later style could support such fierceness (as Beethoven was able to show almost at once), but the discipline of comedy which transformed and enriched Haydn's style left an eradicable impression on his musical personality.[12]

Rosen's description is quite eloquent, yet the stylistic features which he

---

[12]Charles Rosen, The Classical Style: Haydn, Mozart, Beethoven (New York, W.W. Norton, 1971), p. 147.

ascribes to Haydn's Sturm und Drang period, such as "fierce dramatic power," "urgent regularity," and "dazzling eccentricity" are completely undefined. This passage also demonstrates some of the inherent problems in what might be defined as the "traditional" explanation of the musical Sturm und Drang. To begin with, Rosen's description is a resounding affirmation of the notion that Haydn's Sturm und Drang symphonies are entirely sui generis: self-generated, self-contained, and self-extinguished. Secondly, Rosen is very insistent that the Sturm und Drang is an imperfect realization of the potentialities of eighteenth-century harmonic language, the perfect example of which occurred in the High Classic style of Mozart, Haydn, and early Beethoven. However, it is hardly logical to assume that the full potential of any musical language could be fulfilled without stylistic change and development. Rosen seems to regard the Sturm und Drang as a stylistic period preceding the High Classic but without any line of continuity or development between the two. Thirdly, Rosen's assertion that the "discipline of comedy" radically altered Haydn's symphonic writing in his later years will not stand up to scrutiny. It is hardly accurate to state that Symphony No. 94 ("Surprise") of 1791 contains any more comedy or wit than the Sturm und Drang Symphony No. 45 ("Abschied") of 1772.

    Jens Peter Larsen is similarly ambivalent about the musical nature of the Sturm und Drang symphonies. While denying any relationship between the Sturm und Drang symphonies and the literary Sturm und Drang (which would seem to place the symphonies within the general context of Haydn's orchestral output taken as a whole), and naming no specific musical effects except the use of minor keys, Larsen states in The New Grove Haydn that in the Sturm und Drang symphonies Haydn "tackled entirely new problems of form, style and expression."[13] In many respects, then, Larsen is following the same approach as Lang and Rosen, namely, that the *Sturm und Drang* symphonies of Haydn represent a self-contained, completely original style of unspecific musical characteristics which is closely identified with either the literary movement of the same name or the European *Zeitgeist* of the 1770s, and generating little or no influence upon future musical developments.

Some musicologists have tried to remove the *Sturm und Drang* symphonies of Haydn from the debate concerning the influence of the literary *Sturm und Drang* upon the music of the middle eighteenth century, while at the same time insisting that these symphonies represent a completely unique style. One such scholar is Carolyn D. Gresham whose article "Stylistic Features of Haydn's Symphonies from 1768 to 1772" is an attempt to portray the supposedly original features of the *Sturm und Drang* from a musical, instead of a literary or dramatic, standpoint. Gresham begins the article with the following statement: "The period from 1768 to 1772 represents a unique, isolated phase in Joseph Haydn's symphonic output."[14] Referring to the *Sturm und Drang* period as the "Expansive Period," she lists twelve expressive characteristics of the symphonies from this period in addition to the heightened presence of the minor mode: abrupt changes in dynamics, continuous *Fortspinnung* phrases, expressive appoggiaturas, disjunct melodies, dramatic repeated notes, suspensions, syncopation, pedals for phrase

---

[13] Jens Peter Larsen, *The New Grove Haydn* (New York: W.W. Norton, 1983), p. 29.

[14] Carolyn D. Gresham, "Stylistic Features of Haydn's Symphonies from 1768 to 1772," in *Haydn Studies*, eds. Jens Peter Larsen, Howard Serwer, and James Webster (New York: W.W. Norton, 1981), p. 431.

extension, silence, contrasts of timbre, tremolos, and deceptive cadences.[15] This would appear to limit their appropriateness as determining factors of a completely unique musical style. In addition, Gresham contradicts herself and effectively negates her argument when at the concluding portion of her article she states: "Many of these features can also be found in earlier and later Haydn symphonies."[16] Her final characterization of Haydn's symphonic development is that the pre-1768 symphonies are predictable (hence undramatic), the "Expansive" symphonies are unpredictable (hence dramatic), and the post-1772 symphonies are a reversion to a simpler, more popular style.[17]

There are several inherent problems with Gresham's analysis. To begin with, it is very ironic that someone who set out to define Haydn's symphonic style ca. 1768-1772 without using the subjective criteria of the traditional Sturm und Drang interpretation ended up reiterating the traditional definition of the Sturm und Drang, especially its unpredictability and dramatic power, both of which are highly subjective in nature. Secondly, Gresham is concerned with the 1768-1772 period of Haydn's symphonic activity to the extent that the rest of his symphonies seem almost anonymous. It is unfair to detail minutely one style and then to contrast that style with others which are presented in only the barest of outlines. Thirdly, and most significantly, by referring to the Sturm und Drang as the "Expansive" period, Gresham has added another term of jargon to a subject already replete with

---

[15]Ibid., p. 433.

[16]Ibid.

[17]Ibid., pp. 433-434.

jargon. The choice of the term "Expansive" is also unfortunate in that, by definition, it effectively eliminates consideration of any musical details in which the Sturm und Drang might represent a retrenchment or contraction of earlier practices.

Those scholars who make detailed claims for the Sturm und Drang style of Haydn are by no means in agreement with one another. H. C. Robbins Landon enumerates what is probably the longest and most specific list of musical characteristics in Volume II of Haydn: Chronicle and Works:

(1) preponderance of minor keys
(2) the use of the so-called "sonata da chiesa" format, that is, four movements: slow, fast, slow, fast
(3) increased awareness of contrapuntal forms
(4) use of Gregorian plainchant
(5) increased use of dynamic marks, especially crescendo
(6) use of unison forte opening subjects combined with sharp dynamic contrasts within the main subject
(7) long harmonic lines, particularly in slow movements
(8) use of syncopated rhythmic patterns
(9) wide leaps in thematic material sometimes combined with longer than usual note values
(10) increased orchestration
(11) increase in musical humor[18]

Before examining the suitability of any of these stylistic criteria, it is necessary and especially enlightening to compare Landon's list with those of four different scholars: Barry S. Brook, Leonard Ratner, Karl Geiringer, and Friedrich Blume.

---

[18]Landon, Chronicle, 2: 273-278.

In a thought-provoking essay entitled "Sturm und Drang and the Romantic Period in Music," Barry S. Brook defines eight attributes of the Sturm und Drang style:

(1) preoccupation with the minor mode
(2) driving, syncopated rhythms
(3) melodic motives built on wide leaps
(4) harmonies full of tension
(5) pointed dissonances
(6) extended modulations
(7) greater breadth of dynamics and accentuation
(8) fascination with contrapuntal devices[19]

This list is very similar to Landon's, as would be expected considering that both scholars share virtually the same opinion as to the origin of the Sturm und Drang style. Brook, however, conspicuously omits several of the attributes contained in Landon's list.

Karl Geiringer details four specific components of the Sturm und Drang style in his book Haydn: A Creative life in Music: minor keys, contrapuntal devices, more explicit markings of dynamics and a tendency to use unison material at the beginnings of movements.[20] In addition, in a manner somewhat paralleling the literary approach of Paul Henry Lang, Geiringer equates the musical Sturm und Drang with "severe dignity,

---

[19]Barry S. Brook, "Sturm und Drang and the Romantic Period in Music," Studies in Romanticism 9 (1970): 269-284.

[20]Karl Geiringer, Haydn: A Creative Life in Music, 3rd. ed. (Berkeley: University of California Press, 1982), pp. 252ff.

passionate fervor and dramatic intensity."[21] Friedrich Blume describes the Sturm und Drang symphonies of Haydn in a disturbingly self-contradictory way. In Classic and Romantic Music, Blume states that these symphonies:

> ...*form an isolated group in Haydn's work* and no apparent path leads from them to the Romantic era....In choice of tonalities, rhythmic excitement, tense thematic work, motivic texture, predilection for unisons and harmonic jolts, *these Haydn symphonies of around 1770* (whatever the reason for their being so constructed) *anticipate much that we hear again in Beethoven.*[22] [Italics mine.]

The most engaging analysis of the Sturm und Drang within the context of the classical era is contained in Leonard Ratner's Classic Music: Expression, Form and Style. In this book Ratner lists the following characteristics of the musical Sturm und Drang:

(1) driving rhythms
(2) full texture
(3) minor mode melodies
(4) chromaticism
(5) sharp dissonances
(6) impassioned style of declamation[23]

---

[21]Ibid., p. 259.

[22]Friedrich Blume, Classic and Romantic Music (New York: W.W. Norton, 1970), p. 101.

[23]Leonard Ratner, Classic Music: Expression, Form and Style (New York: Schirmer Books, 1980), p. 21. Ratner's analysis of the Sturm und Drang is extremely significant in that he is one of the few scholars to admit traces of this style in the later works of Haydn. Ratner makes a very detailed analysis of Haydn's Symphony No. 102, in which he claims that the sforzandi, tremolos, and appoggiaturas of measures 191-202 of this symphony's first movement are

Minor modality is the only trait held in common in the analyses of the musical <u>Sturm und Drang</u> by the five aforementioned authors, although the rhythmic stresses of the style are noted by all, but not in any consistent manner. Several of the authors (Landon, Brook, and Geiringer) mention the preponderance of contrapuntal devices, specifically those of the baroque, as a leading style characteristic of this music. Yet it is hardly logical for those who consider the <u>Sturm und Drang</u> to be so radically different from the music that preceded it to assume that baroque counterpoint would be a major characteristic of what, from their perspective, would be the musical avant-garde of the 1770s. This would seem to be an anachronistic, rather than progressive, feature.

Landon makes several claims for the musical <u>Sturm und Drang</u> which receive no support from any other scholars. First is his assertion that the use of Gregorian chant is a characteristic of the style in general. Since Landon can only cite the examples of Symphony No. 26 ("Lamentatione") and the Trio of Symphony No. 45 ("Abschied"), given the fact that there were eighteen

---

remnants of the <u>Sturm und Drang</u> style.

There are, however, two problems with Ratner's analysis. Firstly, his details are derived from contemporary eighteenth- and nineteenth-century theoretical sources which are then applied to the compositions in question. In other words, secondary source materials determine the points of analysis of the primary materials. Secondly, what Ratner decides is a <u>Sturm und Drang</u> element in a given work is largely a matter of subjective interpretation. Ratner's description of the <u>Sturm und Drang</u> is very closely related to his description of the <u>Empfindsamkeit</u>, namely, "rapid changes in mood, broken figures, interrupted continuity, elaborate ornamentation, pregnant pauses, shifting, uncertain, often dissonant harmonies--all qualities suggesting intense personal involvement, forerunners of romantic expression, and directly opposed to the statuesque beauty of baroque music" (p. 22).

symphonies composed by Haydn during the 1766-1772 period, it is hardly valid that this is characteristic of the style in general. Additionally, there is a pre-Sturm und Drang symphony, No. 30 ("Alleluja") from 1765 which employs the Alleluia melody for Holy Week in its first movement. Undoubtedly, this use of chant fulfills an extramusical or symbolic purpose and, like the famous adagio finale of Symphony No. 45, serves no noticeable logic of formal construction.

Another point of Landon's that is easily refutable is the claim that the sonata da chiesa form is a normal component of the Sturm und Drang symphonies. Out of the entire body of Haydn symphonies only seven follow to one degree or another the slow-fast-slow-fast movement outline that is the most important musical trait of the sonata da chiesa: six predate the Sturm und Drang (Nos. 5, 11, 18, 21, 22, and 34). What is particularly interesting is that while Landon feels that Symphony No. 44 ("Trauer") displays the influence of the sonata da chiesa,[24] even though the work begins with a movement whose tempo marking is allegro con brio, there is only one Sturm und Drang symphony that actually begins with a slow movement, Symphony No. 49 ("La Passione"). It would appear, therefore, that the sonata da chiesa format was found most often before the Sturm und Drang and was gradually abandoned by Haydn.

Nowhere does the stylistic confusion surrounding the Sturm und Drang become more apparent than in regard to orchestration. Concerning Haydn's Symphony No. 45, Landon implies that this work uses an expanded

---

[24]Landon, Chronicle, 2: 297-298. "Here Haydn finally achieved the form he had sought so long, for the emotional world of the sonata da chiesa was successfully transfered to the normal symphonic structure."

orchestration over that found in the earlier symphonies,[25] while Geiringer views the small orchestra of this work as indicative of a process of simplification resulting from a Rousseauian "back to nature impulse."[26] Comparing the score of Symphony No. 45 to earlier works reveals, however, little or no change in orchestration. The orchestration of No. 45 is composed of two oboes, bassoon, two horns, and strings, which is precisely the same orchestra as that used in all of the Fürnberg-Morzin symphonies. Clearly, it is not until the final third of Haydn's career, especially in those works written for foreign commissions, that he begins to expand significantly the orchestration of his symphonic compositions on a regular basis to include simultaneous flutes, oboes, and clarinets and the conspicuous presence of tympani.

Another claim by Landon for the Sturm und Drang, namely, that the style is marked by a new sense of long harmonic lines, especially in the slow movements, "where one sometimes has the impression that time seems to stand still,"[27] seems to be rather far-fetched. Landon quotes measures 162-181 from the second movement of Symphony No. 45 (without indicating their placement within the movement) as one of two supporting examples. Although the modulations in this passage are unusual for the time, it is necessary to keep in mind that nowhere in Landon's quotation does the harmonic rhythm remain unchanged for more than two measures. It is unclear as to how Landon perceives so little impetus in the harmonic line.

---

[25]Ibid., 2: 278.

[26]Geiringer, Haydn, p. 261.

[27]Landon, Chronicle, 2: 273.

Without citing any specific passages, the slow movement of Symphony No, 54 is also proffered by Landon as evidence for his claim, which is curious because this symphony is not normally associated with the Sturm und Drang (which seems to invalidate its usefulness in this context).

Haydn, however, was writing with long harmonic lines in a manner suggesting temporal stasis well before the Sturm und Drang. The opening passage of the second movement of Symphony No. 10 displays the expansion of the harmonic line, whereby the simple progression of tonic-dominant-tonic occurs over eleven measures at an andante tempo. In the passage just mentioned the static nature of the first violin and cello/bass lines tend to belie the rhythmic impulse of the inner lines and suggests a period of temporal suspension. Obviously, Haydn was aware of the musical effects of long and slow harmonic lines from the very first years of his creative life. This is hardly a unique feature of the Sturm und Drang.

Equally suspicious is the contention of both Landon and Blume that unison and forte opening subjects are a peculiarity of the Sturm und Drang style. While this is true of some of these symphonies (especially No. 44, movement one), it is not true of all of Haydn's Sturm und Drang symphonies. Nor was the use of unison and forte opening subjects limited to the Sturm und Drang alone. In a very fascinating early work, Symphony No. 2, Haydn was already most definitely utilizing these devices. (See Symphony No. 2:1, mm. 1-7.)

The "motivic texture" of the Sturm und Drang symphonies alluded to by Friedrich Blume does not seem to be any more characteristic of these works than for the other periods of Haydn's symphonic output. Karl Geiringer eloquently details the motivic nature of both the Sturm und Drang and earlier symphonies:

> Haydn's tendency to unify certain movements of his works, so obvious in most types of his instrumental output, is developed with particular strength in his symphonies. Apart from the predilection for contrapuntal forms mentioned before, occasionally--as in the first movement of No. 28 [ca. 1765]--a whole movement in sonata form grows out of a single motive. The tendency of the mature Haydn to develop the subsidiary theme out of the main idea is already noticeable; in the first movement of No. 39 [Sturm und Drang work], for instance, the contrasting idea appears only in the epilogue. In the finale of No. 36 [ca. 1762], Haydn was so eager to give thematic material even to the accompanying parts that his exposition assumed certain aspects of a development; accordingly, the real development seems all but superfluous and is six bars in length.[28]

The idea of motivic development and unity extends throughout Haydn's career. In his later years there is even evidence to suggest that motivic construction becomes not merely a localized concerned within a single movement or multi-movement work, but even within groups of compositions. In the London symphonies, which are prime examples of mature classic construction with contrasting themes, there are remarkable motivic ideas held in common among different works. As an example of this phenomenon, there is a close affinity between the opening canzona-like motives of the main sections of the first movements of Symphonies 99 and 100. (See Symphony No. 99:1, mm. 19-24 and Symphony No. 100:1, mm. 24-31.) "Motivic texture," therefore, is an apt description not only of the Sturm und Drang but of almost

---

[28]Geiringer, Haydn, pp. 237-238.

every phrase of Haydn's symphonic writing from the 1750s to the 1790s.

The use of syncopated rhythms has been suggested as a feature of the Sturm und Drang, especially by Landon and Brook. In addition, almost every other commentator on this subject makes some mention of the rhythmic forcefulness that is supposedly peculiar to the Sturm und Drang. Some of Haydn's symphonies from this period do display a great deal of syncopation, particularly Nos. 45 and 49. Other symphonies, such as No. 43 display very little syncopation, while No. 44 contains no syncopated passages lasting more than two measures. Syncopation, however, is used frequently by Haydn in symphonies before and after the Sturm und Drang. A most remarkable instance of this is the second movement of Symphony No. 4 in which syncopation occurs throughout the entire movement. Similarly, in Haydn's final symphony, No. 104, syncopation is employed to great effect. In the first movement of this work, after the introduction, the statement of the first theme contains a syncopated countermelody that provides most of the movement's rhythmic propulsion. (See Symphony No. 104:1, mm. 17-31.)

Undoubtedly, the single most impressive piece of evidence to support the theory that the Sturm und Drang symphonies of Haydn are of a completely unique style is the very small number of symphonies in minor keys that were composed during the eighteenth century and their concentration within a very short period of time. This was noticed by Landon as early as 1956 in his article "La crise romantique dans la musique autrichienne vers 1770":

> This is the idea of the minor mode in the works of Carl Philipp Emanuel Bach who remained strongly attached to the preceding era, while Southern Europe had for a long while succumbed to the light pleasures of the new style. Outside of the works of C. P. E. Bach, minor-keyed symphonies were very

rare. In The Thematic Catalogue of 18th Century Symphonies established by Professor Jan LaRue and myself, which at this time lists 7000 symphonies, not even a fiftieth--that is to say, around 140--are in minor keys. Among these 7000 symphonies only one is in f# minor, the "Farewell" No. 45 of Haydn.[29]

This idea is seized by Brook in his 1970 article "Sturm und Drang and the Romantic Period in Music":

> The use of the minor key as the principal tonality in the instrumental music of the eighteenth century was extremely rare, and it almost invariably had special meaning. It must be considered the sine qua non for a Sturm und Drang piece. Furthermore, around 1770 works that were in minor were almost invariably Sturm und Drang in character. In the symphony, only 2 to 3 percent of the perhaps 20,000 known works in this genre are in minor (the ratio is higher in France, but even there falls short of 9 percent).[30]

---

[29]H. C. Robbins Landon, "La crise romantique dans la musique autrichienne vers 1770," in Les influences étrangères dans l'oeuvre de W. A. Mozart, ed. Andre Verchaly (Paris: Editions du Centre Nationale de la Recherche Scientifique, 1958), p. 31.

Telle est la conception du mode mineur dans les oeuvres de Carl Philipp Emanuel Bach qui demeurait fortement attaché a l'ére précédente, tandis que l'Europe de Sud avait succombé depuis longtemps aux légers plaisirs du nouveau style. En dehors des oeuvres de C.P.E. Bach, les symphonies en mineur sont de plus rares. Le catalogue thématique des Symphonies du XVIIIe siècle, établi par le professeur Jan LaRue et moi-même, réunit jusqu'à présent 7000 symphonies, dont pas même un ciquantième--c'est-à-dire environ 140--sont dans les tonalities mineurs. Parmi ces 7000 symphonies une seule est en fa dièse mineur, Les Adieux no 45 de Haydn.

[30]Brook, "Sturm und Drang," p. 278.

There does, however, seem to be a considerable amount of evidence to suggest that the great frequency of occurrence of the minor mode in those compositions designated as part of the Sturm und Drang, may, in fact, be due to long-established musical procedures rather than a component of a completely unique musical style. One very appealing argument is that of Joel Kolk, who believes that the increased use of the minor mode in the Sturm und Drang was heavily influenced by the practices found in contemporary operatic activity.[31] Kolk's thesis, found in his article "Sturm und Drang and Haydn's Opera," centers on three points: (1) Haydn's operatic activity at Esterhaza began at approximately the same time as the initial appearance of the Sturm und Drang symphonies; (2) Haydn's comic operas made the same limited use of the minor mode as did those of his contemporaries; and (3) as Haydn's operatic activity broadened, there was no overt increase in his use of the minor mode.[32]

Although Kolk only defines the Sturm und Drang in terms of its employment of the minor mode, if his theory is correct, it effectively removes the linchpin of the traditional theory of the musical Sturm und Drang. If the use of minor tonalities in the Sturm und Drang symphonies is a consequence of operatic practices, then it would hardly be accurate to consider these symphonies as belonging to anything but an evolving orchestral style--a midpoint, as it were (but closely related to its preceding point), in Haydn's symphonic development. Likewise, if Haydn's operatic output is within the

---

[31]Joel Kolk, "Sturm und Drang and Haydn's Opera," in Haydn Studies, eds. Jens Peter Larsen, Howard Serwer, and James Webster (New York: W.W. Norton, 1981), pp. 440-445.

[32]Ibid., p. 440.

usual pattern of eighteenth-century practices (which it assuredly is), then the Austrian or European "crisis" of Landon and Brook can be explained as simply an opera-influenced awareness of emotional and rhetorical expressiveness that was reached by many composers at roughly the same period of time. It would seem more logical to assume that operatic practices would be precipitating factors in the development of orchestral music rather than the literary <u>Sturm und Drang</u>, the works of which appeared, almost without exception, following the so-called musical <u>Sturm und Drang</u>. Kolk summarizes his findings as follows:

> This evidence suggests that around 1770, opera composers reserved the minor mode and an accompanying repertory of musical effects for rhetorical accompaniments to moments of heightened tension and occasionally for the representation of storms. Since Haydn used the minor mode in this way in his operas, it seems unlikely that his use of similar materials in instrumental music represented an involuntary response to extramusical influence.[33]

Another very good explanation of the use of the minor keys in opposition to that proffered by the traditional interpreters of the <u>Sturm und Drang</u> is that many of these works have explicit or implicit programmatic connotations, with the choice of key more likely to be the result of selection within an established system of key aesthetics rather than a desire on the part of the composer to use a particular tonality for its shock value. Four out of the six of Haydn's minor-keyed <u>Sturm und Drang</u> symphonies have such programmatic features: No. 49 ("La Passione"), No. 26 ("Lamentatione"), No.

---

[33]Ibid., p. 445.

44 ("Trauer"), and No. 45 ("Abschied"). In a very original and thorough contribution to the study of key aesthetics entitled <u>A History of Key Characteristics in the Eighteenth and Early Nineteenth Centuries</u>, Rita Steblin has collated practically every known statement made by eighteenth- and nineteenth-century musicians, writers, and aestheticians on the qualities and characteristics of each tonality. What becomes clear from Steblin's examination of key aesthetics is that each of the four minor-keyed symphonies with programmatic titles mentioned above was composed in a tonality that was very appropriate for its programmatic content, and that each tonality had a long-established tradition of characteristics.[34]

Additional problems come to the fore in dealing with the musical <u>Sturm und Drang</u> other than the profound disagreement as to its musical features. As has been mentioned earlier in this chapter under the heading "Historiography," the antagonism that exists between the proponents of a cultural/intellectual approach to the <u>Sturm und Drang</u> controversy and those favoring an analytical approach accounts, in large part, for the unresolved nature of the controversy itself. One such area in which the split between the cultural/intellectual historical approach and analytical approach is very apparent is the great concern shown by the former group for the <u>Zeitgeist</u>. Even when the term <u>Zeitgeist</u> is not directly employed it often makes its presence strongly felt in discussions of the musical <u>Sturm und Drang</u>. When we consider that the term <u>Sturm und Drang</u> was not used to describe a musical style until 1909, and then was appropriated from literary criticism, it

---

[34]Rita Steblin, <u>A History of Key Characteristics in the Eighteenth and Early Nineteenth Centuries</u> (Ann Arbor: UMI Research Press, 1983), pp. 242, 257, 265, and 272.

is very clear that from its inception as a style category the musical Sturm und Drang was centered on the idea of the Zeitgeist.[35]

There are three major problems associated with the emphasis placed upon the Zeitgeist by cultural/intellectual historians. (1) In looking upon a specific musical work (or group of works) as representative of a pan-artistic style or cultural epoch, there is the very prevalent tendency for the metaphor to be construed as a metonymy. In other words, a composition which is seemingly related in spirit and/or construction to a general artistic style is viewed not as a parallel or similar phenomenon, but as a direct objectification of that style. (2) Inherently, the Zeitgeist (and by extension, the term Sturm und Drang) perpetuates the pernicious and completely unjustified notion that music always follows the advances made by the other arts. (3) In attempting to link artistic phenomena to the Zeitgeist, cultural/intellectual historians often have recourse to the dubious methodologies of psychohistory and psychobiography. Wyzewa himself first sought the origin of Haydn's minor-keyed symphonies in the composer's unhappy marital situation before suggesting the literary Sturm und Drang as a possible source of inspiration.

Additionally, Zeitgeist is a term that is so amorphous that its mutability provides an extremely strong defense against criticism. It is very difficult to oppose an intellectual concept that cannot be defined unequivocally. While musical analysis tends to be factual, albeit on a microcosmic level, cultural/intellectual history is usually macrocosmic in conception, thereby allowing its adherents to cull supporting evidence from a wide variety of

---

[35]See in particular, Max Rudolf, "Storm and Stress in Music, Part II," Bach: The Quarterly Journal of the Riemenschneider Bach Institute 3 (July 1972): 3-6.

scholarly endeavors. More importantly, proponents of the Zeitgeist are able to make sweeping generalizations from little or no data, resulting in statements that often seem contrary to the facts, or based upon a line of post hoc reasoning. A perfect case in point is Barry S. Brook's assertion that:

> There may be no evidence whatever that Haydn read Rousseau, Lavater, Mercier, Herder or Goethe, but I find it impossible to believe that he could have been insensitive to the widespread distress, disenchantment and melancholy that were in the air of Europe at the time.[36]

Another problem of historiography that definitely colors one's interpretation of the musical Sturm und Drang is the division of eighteenth-century music into distinctive style periods, each of which having more or less defined temporal parameters and assigned in a chronological order from the late baroque to the late classic. Larsen sets forward the following categories: "I Late Baroque, until about 1740; II Midcentury Style, ca. 1740-1770; III Classical style, ca. 1770-1800; and IV Early Romanticism, from about 1800."[37] Friedrich Blume is even more specific in this regard, listing the order of classical styles: galant, Empfindsamkeit, Sturm und Drang, and high classic.[38] Even though both scholars are quick to point out that there is a

---

[36]Brook, "Sturm und Drang," p. 278.

[37]Jens Peter Larsen, "Some Observations on the Development of Viennese Classical Music," Studia Musicologica 9 (1967): 123.

[38]Blume, Classic, pp. 30-31.

great amount of confusion regarding these various style categories,[39] assigning an order and/or time limit suggests that one style necessarily evolved out of another and that, mutatis mutandis, the rate and degree of style evolution was relatively uniform throughout Western civilization.

There exists, however, a considerable amount of evidence to suggest that the terms galant and Empfindsamkeit were defined by eighteenth- and nineteenth-century critics and aestheticians in much the same way that twentieth-century musicologists have defined the term Sturm und Drang. Similarities between the descriptions of the Empfindsamkeit and the Sturm und Drang have already been mentioned above;[40] however, what is particularly intriguing are the similarities of description which seem to exist between the galant and the Sturm und Drang. According to aestheticians of the galant such as Georg Simon Löhlein and Johann Adolph Scheibe, the galant style in music was characterized by the qualities of ambiguity, strange mixtures of compositional techniques, an emphasis on emotional content, the free handling of dissonances, leaping to and from dissonances, and modulations to remote key areas.[41] All of these characteristics have at one time or another been used to describe the musical Sturm und Drang. Taken as a whole, they present an outline of a musical style that is very similar

---

[39]Larsen is especially careful in this regard to point out conflicting usages of not only Sturm und Drang, but galant, rococo, and Empfindsamkeit as well. See Larsen, "Some Observations," pp. 121-122.

[40]See, in particular, footnote 24 of this chapter.

[41]For additional information on the galant, particularly in regard to its conflicting meanings, see David A. Sheldon's excellent article, "The Galant Style Revisited and Re-evaluated," Acta Musicologica 47 (1975): 240-270.

indeed to what has been termed the Sturm und Drang, which was supposedly a later stylistic development than the galant.

This tends to support the idea that there was a great deal of fluidity among the various style categories of the classical era and that these were by no means completely sequential phenomena. Ironically, Wyzewa's statement about Haydn's output after 1772, "... mais c'est depuis lors que Joseph Haydn nous apparaît employant son génie au service de ce style nouveau de musique 'galant,'"[42] begins to take on more of an aura of veracity, even though the reference to a "new" galant style is hardly historically correct.

The basic question as to whether the musical Sturm und Drang was a completely unique style, an intensification of contemporary styles, or was nonexistent still remains to be answered. The preceding chapter has been an attempt to put the debate and its implications in sharper focus and to point out the inconsistencies in terminology and definitions of previous writers on the subject. The next three chapters constitute an effort to define, if possible, the musical Sturm und Drang as evidenced in Haydn's symphonic output.

---

[42]Wyzewa, "A Propos," p. 943.

CHAPTER II

FORM

> Further, the many things, we say, can be seen but are not objects of rational thought whereas the forms are objects of thought but invisible.
> -----Plato, <u>The Republic</u>, 507b

Introduction

Formal structures in eighteenth-century music are largely outlines of standardized harmonic progressions which define limitations of tonality. Even though motivic manipulation and development are important phenomena occurring in this music, their effects are localized in nature, being more a function of the various compositional procedures involved rather than overall formal structure. The seemingly universal stylistic quality (or generic nature) of classic music results, therefore, from its adherence to plans of tonality which engender a series of anticipated tonal digressions.

Chief among these plans of tonality in the eighteenth century were the various sonata forms. Since sonata form calls for alternating periods of defined harmonic stasis and undefined harmonic instability, it would be logical to assume (and is certainly supported by the preponderance of the extant musical evidence) that its defined segments are relatively uniform in overall structure (i.e., tonal outline) from work to work and composer to composer. Differences and/or similarities, therefore, will be most apparent in those segments of sonata form in which the composer was relatively free from tonal strictures. As a result of this, the present study will primarily concern itself, when it is confronted with sonata form, with those areas of harmonic instability. These areas, in declining order of importance, are:

>(1) <u>development</u>--The development is by definition an area of harmonic freedom and instability. Differences and/or similarities among individual symphonies will be easily recognizable in this area because there are few musical factors present which are catalysts to conformity.
>(2) <u>secondary development</u>--This is an optional area of the recapitulation in which usually the subdominant is emphasized.
>(3) <u>introductions</u>--These will occur specifically before the exposition proper.

Fürnberg-Morzin Symphonies

The first of the Fürnberg-Morzin works, Symphony No. 1 in D major, is the epitome of simplicity of symphonic sonata form construction. The first movement of this work contains a development section of only eighteen measures in length, of which the only tonal levels of importance touched upon are the dominant, supertonic, and point of furthest remove (in this case, vi, at mm 55).¹ The approach to the point of furthest remove is effected through the use of sequence patterns. Haydn's first symphonic movement, therefore, was highly epigonic in structure and contained only enough details to be considered a complete sonata form with development. The remaining two movements do not contain developments.

The next work in this series, Symphony No. 37 in C major, represents a vast increase in formal complexity over that of its predecessor. The first movement, a full sonata form with development, has a development of sixty measures in length, well over one third of the movement. The most interesting feature of this particular movement is the presence of two false reprises as generative structures (at measures 82 and 108-109). The first is overtly a false reprise; the second is masked to a certain extent at measures 108-109 as a V42-I6 cadence. The emphasis that Haydn placed upon the false reprise is noteworthy in that it was an effective means to increase the length and tonal dimensions of the development section. It is also significant that the false reprise was used in such a sophisticated manner in this symphony which was only Haydn's second foray into the symphonic genre. This type of generative structure is something more closely associated with Haydn's middle and late periods of composition and tends to suggest that there is more consistency in formal design throughout Haydn's career than was formerly thought.

---

[1]The point of furthest remove (PFR) is described by Leonard Ratner in <u>Classic Music: Expression, Form and Style</u>, pp. 225-228 as "generally a cadence on a <u>modal</u> degree--III, VI or V of VI.... Its placement is optional at <u>any</u> point within the development.... While the point of furthest remove itself was an <u>option</u> in the development, most sonata forms took advantage of the leverage it provided to give an additional thrust to the harmony."

Movement three of Symphony No. 37, Haydn's first symphonic movement in a minor key, is a very good example of the problems encountered in adapting eighteenth-century formal patterns to minor-keyed movements. The mediant relationship between the tonic key and the point of furthest remove is negated in the development because it is precisely this relationship that is actively pursued in the exposition of a minor-keyed sonata form movement. The only other alternatives for the point of furthest remove, VI or V of VI, are generally employed in a less abrupt manner than the mediant or submediant in a development section of a major-keyed sonata form. In other words, the harmonic impetus of a minor-keyed sonata form movement is generally less dynamic and purposeful than its major-keyed counterpart. The development of movement three begins in the mediant, immediately proceeds to the submediant, and then has very little harmonic direction until the presence of the dominant in measure 43. (See Symphony No. 37:3, mm. 19-46.) The resolution of the harmonic problems inherent in minor-keyed sonata form movements occupied much of Haydn's time in the succeeding decade (i.e., the 1770s). What is important to remember, however, is that the questions themselves had been raised at an earlier date.

The next Fürnberg-Morzin symphony, No. 18 in G major, is extremely simple in formal construction with none of its three movements possessing a full development section. Its real significance, however, rests in the fact that it was composed at approximately the same time as the relatively sophisticated Symphony No. 37 (ca. 1758). Haydn, therefore, utilized both relatively complex and simple formal designs within a short time span. Obviously, the function (setting, place of performance, patron, and performers) of a work of music determined in large part its form. This leads one to surmise that the various types of forms (especially the various approaches to sonata form) were relatively stable by the middle of the eighteenth century and were employed whenever it was deemed appropriate by the composer. The concept of formal evolution in Haydn's symphonic music does not appear to be supported by the plethora of formal schema, ranging from the naive to the sophisticated, which were used by the composer in his earliest works in the genre.

Symphony No. 2 in C major is a fascinating work and displays many interesting formal ideas heretofore not seen. The development section of movement one is quite large (64 measures) and is sustained by the generative force of a number of sequence patterns. The sequence patterns are interrupted by a false reprise which occurs approximately halfway through the development (in measure 94).

Movement three of Symphony No. 2 is also significant in that it is one of the first mature rondos composed by Haydn and is his first symphonic rondo movement. There is a great deal of attention paid to formal balance and symmetry, with an extensive secondary development in F major/minor which balances the G minor "development" (or B) section (measures 57-91).

Symphony No. 15 in D major of the Fürnberg-Morzin series anticipates many of the formal developments usually attributed to Haydn's later stylistic periods. The first movement begins with a slow introduction, a feature that became standard in so-called "sonata-allegro" movements by the time of the composition of the London symphonies. In addition, this movement ends with an adagio, which is a very curious phenomenon, making it more akin to the procedures employed in the finale of Symphony No. 45 than to the group in which it is placed. Like Symphony No. 2, the repeat signs are omitted at the end of the exposition and the tonal level shifts back to the tonic, giving the listener the momentary sensation that the movement is a sonata form without development. Once again, Haydn is toying aurally with his audience in a very sophisticated manner, not merely indicating a false recapitulation, but this time allowing one to believe for a moment that the development will be omitted altogether.

The genius of Haydn's formal structures is revealed not only by those sonata form movements in which a large number of tonal levels is explored, but also by movements in which only a few tonal levels are sufficient to sustain a relatively long sonata form with full development. The first movement of Symphony No. 4 in D major is a case in point. In its development section (24 measures out of a total of 96) only three important tonal levels are touched upon: V, IV, and vi.

Although the classic symphony was conceived as the framework upon which an entire concert was supported and whose movements, like the Ordinary of the Mass, were performed independently rather than successively, Haydn began very early in his symphonic writing to include common elements for all movements of particular symphonies. As mentioned in Chapter I, as early as Symphony No. 2, Haydn had attempted to obscure the binary origins of sonata form by deliberately omitting the repeat signs from all four movements of that symphony. By the time of the composition of Symphony No. 10 in D major, Haydn's attempts at formal unity had assumed a more intellectually formidable façade. The unique feature of Symphony No. 10 is that all three of its movements possess similar sonata forms, namely, that the developments begin in the dominant and then modulate to the tonic with material of the tonic key area. The outward perception, then, is of sonata form without development. This perception is soon obviated because after this has taken place the real development begins in earnest. (Compare Symphony No. 10:1, mm. 1-4 to mm. 38-46; Symphony No. 10:2, mm. 1-6 to mm. 42-54; Symphony No. 10:3, mm. 13-21 to mm. 45-65.) This is a major extension of the idea of the false reprise, coming even before the development has begun. Such a procedure in one movement would be worthy of mention; the fact that it is present in all three movements suggests a conscious determination on the part of the composer to extend formal unification throughout the entire symphony.

After the complicated formal devices employed in Symphony No. 10, Haydn appears to have taken a brief hiatus from the rigorous compositional path that he had laid out before him. His next two symphonies, Nos. 32 in C major and 5 in A major, are a retrenchment in many ways and offer only the most mundane and compact of formal procedures.

The next symphony in chronological order, No. 11 in Eb major, shows Haydn once again to be exploring the numerous subtleties inherent in sonata form. All four movements exhibit the increasing importance attached to the development section, with even the third movement minuet and trio having very short "development" sections in both parts. The first movement adagio is a fascinating study of Haydn's penchant for delaying or negating an anticipated tonal goal. The development section (measures 34-56) studiously avoids both the mediant and submediant, thereby freeing itself of the necessity of a noticeable and abrupt harmonic shift at the point of furthest remove indicating the return of the tonic in the not-too-distant future. The fact that Haydn has dispensed with the point of furthest remove as an harmonic fulcrum allows the movement to unfold in a less purposeful manner than normal and adds to the suspense of the listener attempting to anticipate the recapitulation.

In Symphony No. 33 in C major developmental procedures once again dominate Haydn's symphonic writing. The development section of movement one is particularly impressive, not only in size but in harmonic range as well. This movement is very similar in formal structure to the first movement of a previously mentioned work, Symphony No. 2 (both of which are in C major), in that a fairly rapid harmonic rhythm is present in the development sections of both works. The fact that the same type of developmental procedures are utilized in two symphonies composed in the same key suggests that Haydn's use of sonata form had reached a level of stability at a very early stage in his career. Furthermore, this provides evidence that Haydn in his earliest symphonies was highly sensitive to the aesthetic function of tonality, being consistent not only in evoking similar moods in different works of like tonality, but also in employing similar formal and structural devices.

As has been mentioned earlier in this chapter, in these early symphonies Haydn often followed a formally complex symphony with one or more works of greatly reduced compositional complexity. Being true to form, this situation occurred after the composition of Symphony No. 33. The next two symphonies, Nos. 27 in G major and 107 ("A") in Bb major, while craftsmanlike in their construction, do not approach the level of structural sophistication seen in their immediate predecessor.

The final Fürnberg-Morzin symphony, No. 3 in G major, in many ways is a compendium of the various approaches to formal design that Haydn was experimenting with in his early works. The first and second movements are sonata forms with full developments, typical of these early symphonies, yet a subtle change of Haydn's approach to formal design being detectable in what may seem a relatively unpretentious work. Although the number of tonal levels touched upon in the developments of both movements is nothing out of the ordinary, the amount of time spent in each tonal level is increasing. The second movement, which is only 86 measures in length, contains a development section of 37 measures, or 43% of the entire movement, making it proportionally one of the longest developments to be found anywhere in Haydn's oeuvre. The finale of this work is a finely-developed fugue, serving not only as a consummation of the composer's study of the contrapuntal practices of the baroque, but also as a harbinger of a stylistic feature that many scholars attribute to the Sturm und Drang.

To summarize the formal construction of the Fürnberg-Morzin symphonies a few points should be emphasized. (1) These symphonies display a great variety of sonata forms and a wide diversity of types of formal construction. (2) In the development sections of sonata forms, many tonal levels are touched upon, but none for very long. By the time of Symphony No. 33, however, Haydn was gradually increasing the length of time spent at each tonal level. (3) While Haydn utilizes a large number of sonata form types in these works, it is important to note that the more complex types are present as early as those of little or no formal sophistication. The mature sonata form with full development appears not to have developed out of simpler types, but was present in a mode of relative stability at the very earliest point in Haydn's career. (4) Like the surface details discussed in Chapter I, and following the argument presented in point three above, the formal characteristics of Haydn's later symphonies, with few exceptions, are already present in his Fürnberg-Morzin works.

"Sturm und Drang" Symphonies

As has been discussed in Chapter I, the only important surface detail in which the Sturm und Drang symphonies differ from the rest of Haydn's symphonic output is an increased use of minor keys. This, however, does present some interesting problems of form, specifically, the shape and direction of the harmonic outlines to be followed in the tonally-oriented sonata and rondo forms. Sonata form movements in minor keys, with the emphasis placed upon the tonic-mediant relationship in the exposition, effectively negated the role of the point of furthest remove in the development. This negation is further exacerbated by the dominant relationship between the submediant and the mediant which in this context effectively eliminates the former from consideration as the point of furthest remove. The problem that Haydn and other composers of his generation faced, therefore, was to create in minor-keyed movements the same kind of harmonic direction and impetus that was so readily apparent in their major-keyed works.

The first Sturm und Drang work, Symphony No. 39 in G minor, reveals several of Haydn's attempts at resolving these problems of form. Both the first and fourth movements of this work have development sections that begin in the mediant and then proceed to the subdominant. This pattern will be seen in many of the other symphonic movements in minor keys from this period.

Another procedure used in the fourth movement of Symphony No. 39

is the use of the mediant as a bridge to the dominant in the concluding portion of the movement's development section. The mediant, therefore, does not act as an indication of a sudden harmonic shift, but as a connection to the dominant (which in turn announces the onset of the recapitulation.

Symphony No. 35 in Bb major, the next of the Sturm und Drang works, is composed in a manner very reminiscent of that already seen in the Fürnberg-Morzin symphonies, namely, the use in three movements of full sonata form with development and one movement containing a minuet and trio. On the surface this symphony appears to possess little that is remarkable; however, formally speaking, this work represents a much simpler approach to harmonic development than in the vast majority of Fürnberg-Morzin symphonies. In the development of the first movement, for example, other than the tonic and dominant, only two tonal levels are established (IV and vi, and each of these only once), and long sequential passages link one tonal level to another. This development is much longer than many developments found in Haydn's earlier works which generally employ a larger number of tonal levels. Along with a simplification of sonata form, Haydn experiments with obviating the development with the return of the tonic and then pursuing the development earnestly. In movement four this procedure is followed. Aside from the numerous cases of false reprises and incidental excursions to the tonic in the course of sequence patterns and the like (all of which normally occur toward the middle or end of the development), going to the tonic shortly after the beginning of the development (without the thematic reiteration necessary for a false reprise) is not a new procedure for Haydn. One is directed to Symphony No. 10, movement two and Symphony No. 11, movement one in which the same procedure is followed. The one aspect of Symphony No. 35 that is new is the use of the harmonically-simplified sonata form in movements which are considerably longer than those found in Haydn's earlier orchestral works.

Symphony No. 59 in A major also displays this trend towards simplicity of structure. The development section of the first movement is greatly reduced in length (only twenty nine measures) and, like Symphony No. 35, the tonic is reached before the true development begins.

It has been previously mentioned that a characteristic of Haydn's orchestral writing is that he seems to have pursued a formal idea through two symphonies and then changed to a different method of formal organization. Such is the case with Symphony No. 38 in C major which follows the relatively simple formal schema of Symphonies Nos. 35 and 59. This work contains three movements (one, two, and four) which are full sonata forms with developments. The first movement contains a very long development (mm. 76-131) and, as has been seen in the Fürnberg-Morzin works in the same key of C major, this development touches upon a large number of tonal levels.

Symphony No. 49 in F minor is the first of the three minor-keyed symphonies that inspired Wyzewa to propose the <u>Sturm und Drang</u> as a self-contained stylistic category. Rather than demonstrating a complexity of formal schema as suggested by the canon of the traditional interpretation of the musical <u>Sturm und Drang</u>, Symphony No. 49 is remarkable for the utter simplicity of its formal designs. In the developments of movements one, two, and four only the tonal levels of ii(II), iv, and v(V) are touched upon (beyond expected temporary excursions into the tonic and submediant). The idea of harmonic simplicity is taken up again by Haydn in his next symphony, No. 58 in F major, which is even simpler in formal design than Symphony No. 49.

Only the first movement of this work is a full sonata form with development, and Haydn is able to sustain a development section of forty five measures in length while having recourse to only two tonal levels (V and vi). This development has a highly organized tonal structure, a type of arch form, in which the point of furthest remove occurs at midpoint (F major: V--vi[PFR at measure 73]--V). Regularity of structure, therefore, appears to be the norm rather than an infatuation with the irregular as suggested by the term Sturm und Drang itself.

In Symphony No. 26 in D minor, the D minor minuet section of the third movement demonstrates again the standard practice whereby the mediant appears in the development section (or second reprise in this case) not as the point of furthest remove, but as a link to the dominant. (See Symphony No. 26, movement three, mm. 26-28.) The use of a minuet and trio as the final movement of a three-movement composition is somewhat anachronistic by this time and more clearly represents the format found in early classic sonatas of ca. 1750.

Symphony No. 41 is another of Haydn's C major symphonies. One interesting element of this work is the use of the dominant minor at the beginning of the development section of the first movement. Very clearly, Haydn is beginning to employ the minor mode to greater effect in his major-keyed symphonies which, in reality, is the only musical characteristic of the Sturm und Drang readily accepted by all of the scholars who have previously investigated this matter.

The next symphony in question, No. 48, forms with its predecessor a pair of C major works, one of those pairs of similarly constructed works that constitutes a compositional idiosyncrasy of the composer. Like Symphony No.

41, the first movement of Symphony No. 48 contains a development section more complex than the minor-keyed symphonies of the same period, but not as complex as the C major Fürnberg-Morzin symphonies. The third movement displays larger developmental sections than are normally found in minuets and trios. By far the most interesting and unusual formal structure is found in the fourth movement which contains a development section of only thirteen measures in length, but a secondary development in the recapitulation twenty three measures long. (See Symphony No. 48, movement four, mm. 90-112.) Haydn, therefore, allows the secondary development to function as the true development. Untypical of most secondary developments, the harmonic emphasis is placed upon the supertonic rather than the subdominant; yet, this still acts as a counterbalance to the dominant area of the exposition. More specifically, the secondary development emphasizes the flat side of the circle of fifths (in this case, D minor), while the exposition, of course, stresses the sharp side.

Symphony No. 44 in E minor signals another shift in compositional emphasis and forms yet another pair of similarly constructed works with Symphony No. 52 in C minor. Even though both works are centered in minor keys, the development sections of both works stress very heavily the major mode.

In Symphony No. 43 in Eb major Haydn again concentrates on composing in major keys, a trend that he will continue to follow in the next two succeeding symphonies, Nos. 42 and 51. In the first movement of Symphony No. 43 the composer arrives at the point of furthest remove early in the development (a half authentic cadence in vi at measure 105), and then proceeds to a false reprise at measure 113. This is a particularly important occurrence because up to this time Haydn has not combined an early occurrence of the point of furthest remove with an immediate presentation of a false reprise. The following table indicates those previously discussed symphonies and particular movements in which there has been a false reprise or early point of furthest remove.

TABLE 1

FALSE REPRISES AND EARLY POINTS OF FURTHEST REMOVE

False Reprises	Early Points of Furthest Remove
Fürnberg-Morzin:	Fürnberg-Morzin:
37:1......m. 82	2:1......m. 86
2:1......m. 94	15:1......m. 73
11:2......m. 82	11:4......m. 59
33:1......m. 60	33:1......m. 72
Sturm und Drang:	Sturm und Drang:
41:1......m. 97	38:2......m. 47
43:1......m. 1	43:1......m. 105

The importance given to the false reprise is greatly emphasized by having the point of furthest remove immediately precede it. Haydn, therefore, demonstrates an increasing awareness and facility in manipulating the aural expectations of the listener. The significance of this phenomenon, however, is that it takes place in a major-keyed symphony, which seems to belie the notions that the minor-keyed works are the most dramatically conceived of Haydn's symphonies and that the <u>Sturm und Drang</u> works are essentially revolutionary in construction.

The next symphonies, Nos. 42 in D major and 51 in Bb major, once again demonstrate Haydn's propensity for composing in pairs. In both symphonies the position and function of the movements are alike, even down to very minute details. The first movements of both works utilize false reprises. The false reprise of No. 42, movement occurs very early in the development while that of the first movement of Symphony No. 51 (in the wrong key--Eb major) is delayed until the latter half of the development (mm. 108-109).[2]

Another interesting similarity between Symphonies Nos. 42 and 51 is the use of the rondo in both finales. It is noteworthy that the rondo, a fairly unusual orchestral compositional format until this time, is employed in only two of the symphonies of the <u>Sturm und Drang</u> period and that these are major-keyed symphonies and not their more famous (and supposedly more original) minor-keyed counterparts. The novel use of the rondo form, however, has not escaped Landon's notice. In commenting upon Symphony No. 42 he states:

---

[2]The term "wrong key" false reprise is appropriate here because the section is articulated by a preceding period of silence and contains the only instance here of developmental usage of initial thematic material.

> In the finale Haydn also creates a new and revolutionary form: the characteristic Haydnesque rondo. Perhaps this is the first time it appears, at least in a symphony....[3]

It is hardly accurate to say that the rondo format exhibited in these symphonies is typically "Haydnesque" for the simple reason that the sonata rondo, which appears so prominently in the London symphonies, is a much more stable procedure and seems to have been more favored by the composer than the type of rondo encountered in Symphonies Nos. 42 and 51. Likewise, the "revolutionary" nature of the rondo, as asserted by Landon, is incorrect inasmuch as the rondo made its first appearance in the Fürnberg-Morzin Symphony No. 2, movement four.

Haydn's next Sturm und Drang orchestral work is the well-known and highly discussed Symphony No. 45. The use of the F# minor tonality is unique in the symphonic literature of the classic era; however, from the standpoint of formal design, the work's originality ends here. In the first movement, aside from the mediant, the development section only touches upon four tonal levels: B major/minor, F# major, D major, and G major. The conservative nature of this movement is further demonstrated by the fact that even though it is rooted in a very rare minor key, a large portion of the movement's unfolding takes place in the major mode. This fact, coupled with the small number of tonal levels employed in the development, clearly indicates a condensation and simplification of sonata form (without a concomitant reduction in the size of the movement) when compared to such

---

[3]Landon, Chronicle, II: 301.

earlier works from the <u>Sturm und Drang</u> period as Symphonies No. 38, movement one and 41, movement one, and even the Fürnberg-Morzin Symphonies Nos. 2, movement one and 33, movement one. Larsen's assertion that Haydn resolved entirely new problems of form in the <u>Sturm und Drang</u> works[4] does not seem to be verified by an analysis of these works, especially when the minor-keyed symphonies are compared to their major-keyed counterparts of the same period and the entire corpus of <u>Sturm und Drang</u> symphonies are compared to the earlier body of Fürnberg-Morzin works.

The other notable feature of Symphony No. 45, namely, the famous adagio of the final movement, from which the movement derives its sobriquet, is not an original feature nor is it symptomatic of the <u>Sturm und Drang</u> as a whole. Haydn had employed a simplified version of this procedure as early as the first movement of Symphony No. 15. From an harmonic standpoint, it is vital to recognize the fact that the interpolation of the adagio in the finale of Symphony No. 45 in no way deters the movement from arriving at the tonal goal it would have reached had the tempo and orchestration of the movement proceeded on its original course.

The interpolation of seemingly extraneous material into the body of a movement is a notable feature of Haydn's next work, Symphony No. 46 in B major. The finale of this symphony contains a minuet initiated in the midst of the development which reverts to the original meter and tempo at the recapitulation. Like the finale of Symphony No. 45, this interpolation in no way affects the formal plan of the movement. Again, Haydn is merely working out an idea in a pair of symphonies before turning his attention to

---

[4]Larsen, <u>The New Grove Haydn</u>, p.29.

something else. As mentioned above, the use of interpolations (and slow introductions and conclusions) is not a unique feature of the Sturm und Drang, and is hardly a representative characteristic of this period of the composer's creative life inasmuch as it occurs in only two symphonies. The cautious and conservative nature of Haydn's artistic personality is revealed here by the fact that a compositional device that was employed very early in his career was used so sparingly in the so-called Sturm und Drang period. Ironically, the use of various types of interpolations is a very prominent feature of his London symphonies, which are considered by many scholars to be less revolutionary and more entertaining in nature than the Sturm und Drang works.

The final two Sturm und Drang symphonies, Nos. 47 in G major and 65 in A major, appear on the surface to be not as formally advanced as the minor-keyed works of the group and, to a certain extent, this is the impression given by a cursory listening. The aural effect of these symphonies, however, is belied by highly developed formal structures which operate subtly, just beneath their outward surfaces. The first movement of Symphony No. 47, for example, contains a lengthy and highly condensed development section in which a large number of tonal levels are embraced. The second movement of this work is a theme and variations, by far the simplest classic compositional procedure in terms of formal construction, yet one that played absolutely no part in the Fürnberg-Morzin symphonies which were supposedly of such simple construction. The third movement, the famous minuet and trio al roverso, while containing an interesting approach to thematic arrangement, nevertheless is quite elementary in its formal construction. Haydn is so preoccupied with melodic construction at this point in time that the formal complexity of his work decreases appreciably. The novelty of the retrograde presentation of the melodic line masks an approach to form that is very conservative and runs counter to the thought that musical forms proceed historically from the simple to the complex. The fourth movement presents the point of furthest remove immediately at the beginning of the development, a device already seen in the finale of Symphony No. 46 (measure 72) and a number of other <u>Sturm und Drang</u> and Fürnberg-Morzin works. This device and the simple formal structure of the theme and variations of the second movement are harbingers of Haydn's approach to symphonic writing in his London symphonies. As stylish as these devices may be, they are not from the pen of a revolutionary; on the contrary, they are the result of a meticulous and well-trained craftsman whose aesthetic sensibilities always remained in firm control of his passions.

It is indeed ironic that the final symphony of the <u>Sturm und Drang</u> period is No. 65. Regarding formal design, there is no symphony even of the composer's earliest works in which the simplicity of harmonic structure is so predominant a factor as in No. 65. The one notable formal feature of this work is the large secondary development in its first movement (mm. 83-108) in which the subdominant and its tonicization are emphasized before the final appearance of the tonic (at measure 109). Similar to movement four of Symphony No.48, the secondary development of the first movement of Symphony No. 65 takes the place and function of a remarkably short development section (in this case only eight measures long). Like the other compositional devices and formal designs which appear to be unique to the <u>Sturm und Drang</u>, the expansion of the secondary development has its roots in the Fürnberg-Morzin works, particularly the third movement of Symphony

No. 2. The emphasis placed upon the secondary development rather than the development itself seems to counter one argument made by Paul Henry Lang, namely, that in a Sturm und Drang work gravity and centrality of action rested in the development section, forming, as it were, the "battlefield of thematic struggle."[5]

London Symphonies

The final group of symphonies in this comparison of formal procedures, collectively known as the London symphonies, constitute Haydn's last unified effort at symphonic writing. At this late point in the composer's career a number of compositional procedures become standardized, resulting in a more generic approach to harmonic organization as well as the arrangement of the movements themselves. The overall impression of the London symphonies regarding formal matters is not that of a more advanced or experimental nature, but the final working out of compositional principles first displayed in the Fürnberg-Morzin works and later taken up in the symphonies of the so-called Sturm und Drang period.

With Symphony No. 96 in D major the entire structure of the symphonic genre becomes paradigmatic. All twelve symphonies of this group adhere more or less to the ordering of movements listed below:

(1) full sonata form with slow introduction
(2) theme and variations or ternary form
(3) minuet and trio

---

[5]Lang, Music in Western Civilization, p. 611.

(4) sonata rondo

The only exceptions are: Symphony No. 95, in which the slow introduction is eschewed in its first movement; Symphony No. 99, in which a full sonata form is substituted for the theme and variations usually found in the second movement; and the finales of Symphonies Nos. 98 and 104 which are full sonata forms instead of the customary sonata rondo.

Another interesting feature of the first movement of Symphony No. 96 is the occurrence of the point of furthest remove at the immediate beginning of the development section, a procedure initiated by Haydn in his <u>Sturm und Drang</u> works (specifically, Symphonies Nos. 42:1, 46:4, and 47:4). Besides this instance in Symphony No. 96:1, the same phenomenon occurs in Symphony No. 99, movement one.

Symphony No. 95 in C minor is the only London work in a minor key and is much less complex tonally than the major-keyed London symphonies (the development of the first movement emphasizes only the major dominant, major submediant, and the subtonic), although it is more tonally complex than the minor-keyed <u>Sturm und Drang</u> works. It is also the only London symphony whose initial movement does not include a slow introduction. All of this suggests the idea that the major-keyed symphonies of Haydn are usually of a more complex formal nature than the minor-keyed symphonies regardless of the period in Haydn's career in which they were composed. Major tonalities appear on the whole to support more sustained and tonally complex developments than their minor-keyed counterparts. It has already been mentioned above that the dynamic nature of the point of furthest remove is effectively negated in a minor-keyed sonata form in which the mediant relationship is a necessary function of the exposition. The fact that Haydn chose to omit the slow introduction from only one London symphony (which also happens to be in a minor key) is of some importance as the slow introduction provided an additional harmonic alternative which was easily sustained in major tonalities, but, as the evidence seems to suggest, was too much harmonic interference with the aesthetic effect of the minor mode.[6]

Haydn's approach to formal procedures is highly intriguing in these final symphonies. Overall formal structures are highly rigid, yet there is surprising flexibility within the restrictions of the few formal patterns he pursues. Nowhere is this more evident than in the next two symphonies of this series, Nos. 93 in D major and 94 in G major. A fascinating comparison can be made between the initial movements of these two symphonies. The first movement of Symphony No. 93 has a complicated development section which touches upon no less than five tonal levels. The first movement of Symphony No. 94, on the other hand, is a much simpler affair, yet it has one curious feature, namely, the movement away from the dominant before the beginning of the development section. This vividly reinforces a compositional idiosyncrasy of Haydn wherein an unusual surface detail is compensated by a concomitant decrease in formal complexity. As if to ensure complete

---

[6]It should be kept in mind that three of the major-keyed London works have slow introductions in minor keys (98:1, 101:1, and 104:1) and one slow introduction (96:1) is in a major key but emphasizes the minor. The early appearance of the minor mode seems not to inhibit the form of a major-keyed movement; on the contrary, it seems actually to enhance the scope and architectonics of the form itself. The opposite does not seem to be a possibility for Haydn, and is left for the next generation of composers, as witness the major mode introduction to the minor-keyed first movement of Beethoven's "Kreutzer" Sonata.

consistency, Haydn balances this early removal from the dominant level of the exposition by having the tonic tonality reappear before the reappearance of expository thematic material in the recapitulation. The compositional logic of this movement, therefore, suggests not a "process" of composition but, in reality, a Gestalt. An early permutation of form alters the form of a later portion of the movement, not unlike the stretching of one point on an elastic surface causing an alteration of the surface's entire body.

Symphony No. 98 in Bb major is a rather unusual symphony in that its final movement is more tonally complex than its initial movement. The development of the finale is very long for a movement in this position and is even of greater length (eighty four measures) than the development of the first movement (seventy seven measures).

Symphony No. 97 is of a much simpler formal organization than any of Haydn's other C major symphonies examined previously in this book. The development of the first movement begins with the flat mediant, a displacement of traditional harmonic procedures whereby this tonal level would probably be preceded at some point by the tonic minor. More notable in this movement is the false reprise (at measure 143), which is the only instance in the London series where Haydn employs this particular device. Although the conventional appraisal of the London symphonies assumes an increased preoccupation with harmonic twists and unforeseen recapitulations, in reality, the chief means of providing an unanticipated turn in the unfolding of an eighteenth-century sonata form, namely, the premature recapitulation or false reprise, was employed to a much greater degree in the symphonies of Haydn's Fürnberg-Morzin and Sturm und Drang periods, as the following table indicates.

TABLE 2

FALSE REPRISES AND THEIR TONALITIES

Symphony/movement	Tonality
Fürnberg-Morzin:	
37:1	C major
2:1	C major
11:2	Eb major
33:1	C major
<u>Sturm und Drang</u>:	
41:1	C major
43:1	Eb major
51:1	Bb major [False reprise in wrong key--Eb major]
42:1	D major
46:1	B major

An interesting point brought forward from the table above is that Haydn does not use the false reprise in minor-keyed movements. Generally speaking, he is rather conservative when dealing with unusual tonalities (although an exception might be the false reprise in B major in Symphony No. 46, movement one). Likewise, Haydn seems the most adventurous in formal construction when dealing with a familiar key in the major mode.

The fourth movement of Symphony No. 97 in C major, a C major sonata rondo of quite simple formal design, contains a sizeable section of the recapitulation in the tonic minor. In these late orchestral works Haydn is incorporating minor keys to a greater extent and wider syntax than in his previous major-keyed symphonies or in quite a few of his earlier minor-keyed works. Many of the minor-keyed works of the <u>Sturm und Drang</u> period (e.g., movement one of Symphony No. 45) have development sections in which minor tonal levels are scarcely encountered.

The next symphony in this group, No. 99 in Eb major, places an additional emphasis upon mediant relationships. The key of the second movement is neither in the same key as the first movement (Eb major), nor more typically, a fourth or fifth removed, but is a major third removed (G major). This is a very rare phenomenon up to this period of time (almost as rare as some of the minor-key tonalities in the <u>Sturm und Drang</u> works) and points toward nineteenth-century procedures, especially those of Brahms. In addition, this same type of relationship exists between the Eb major minuet and the C major trio of the symphony's third movement. The dynamism of the mediant is enhanced by a bridge section at the end of the trio (the dominant of the section's C major tonality) that serves as the point of furthest remove for the da capo repeat of the Eb major tonality of the minuet. (See Symphony No. 99, movement three, mm. 101-118.) In seeking to go beyond the standard harmonic formulae that are typical of most minuets and trios, Haydn allows the point of furthest remove to function in its traditional role, thereby effectively linking two keys which are further removed harmonically than what is normally found in similar circumstances.

The next two symphonies, Nos. 100 in G major and 101 in D major, contain few formal devices not already seen in the London symphonies. One important exception is the development section of the first movement of Symphony No. 101 where there is basically a stepwise progression of tonal levels: V, vi, ♭VII, i, ii, and IV.

Symphony No. 102 in Bb major displays an interesting feature typical of the London symphonies, namely, the use of the subtonic as a tonal level of the development section. This occurs in both the first and fourth movements of this work.

The final two symphonies of this series, Nos. 103 in Eb major and 104 in D major, are fascinating in their diverse display of formal procedures. Symphony No. 103 utilizes a large number of sophisticated harmonic devices which are concealed behind an elaborate and deceptively charming façade. The development section of the first movement touches upon four tonal levels: V, ii, vi, and bVII. While this procedure is hardly new to Haydn its importance is that the subtonic level appears in the position normally associated with the point of furthest remove, i.e., immediately before the dominant preparation for the recapitulation's return to the tonic. Haydn clearly is being more flexible with his handling of the various tonalities than in his Fürnberg-Morzin and Sturm und Drang works and feels free, at this stage in his career, to utilize formal devices in keys with which they were not generally associated. In a very subtle way, this is the apotheosis of his lifelong penchant for confounding the aural expectations of the listener.

The second movement of Symphony No. 103 is a variations on two themes (not to be confused with the double variations which is a different form entirely). The importance of this seemingly simple formal structure is that in the regular alternation between the major and minor themes, equal importance is given to both modes; an equality, incidentally, that is not to be found in the Sturm und Drang symphonies in which the minor keys receive so much superficial attention.

Symphony No. 104 is undoubtedly the most heterogeneous of all of Haydn's symphonies as far as formal construction is concerned. On the one hand, the development section of the first movement of this work only touches upon several tonal levels (vi and II); on the other hand, the third movement contains a mediant relationship between the minuet and trio with a bridge section in which the dominant of the trio acts as the point of furthest remove for the tonic of the da capo of the minuet. It is as though Haydn has one foot in the past and one in the future with the harmonic arrangement of this symphony; paying homage to his youth while pointing ahead to harmonic alternatives that will be exploited by future generations of composers. Symphony No. 104 is, in other words, both an aperçu and an agenda for the future, a most appropriate conclusion for such a distinguished career as a symphonic composer.

If there is a conclusion to be derived from this discussion of form it is that there appears to be a steady development of harmonic procedures from the Fürnberg-Morzin symphonies to those of the London period. The Sturm und Drang symphonies do not possess any unique approaches to form in contrast to what the traditional interpretation of this period would lead us to believe. In fact, almost without exception, the formal procedures employed in the Sturm und Drang works have their origins in the Fürnberg-Morzin works and are continued in the London symphonies. The portrayal of the Sturm und Drang symphonies as sui generis does not hold up to analysis, at least in regard to considerations of form.

While there is an increase in the overall length of Haydn's symphonies the proportion of the lengths of the development sections to the movements in which they are contained is relatively constant; in fact, there is a slight decrease for the Sturm und Drang works. This suggests two ideas: (1) that Haydn's approach to sonata form was standardized by the time of his earliest period of compositional activity, and (2) that the Sturm und Drang symphonies do not represent a greater complexity of formal procedures; on the contrary, in the area of greatest harmonic freedom, namely, the development, the Sturm und Drang symphonies are more conservative than their predecessors. The following table illustrates this point

TABLE 3

COMPARISON OF FULL SONATA FORM DEVELOPMENTS TO THE MOVEMENTS IN WHICH THEY OCCUR EXCLUSIVE OF VARIATIONS, RONDOS, MINUETS AND TRIOS, FUGUES/FUGATOS, AND TERNARY FORMS

Symphony/Movement	mm. in mvt.	mm. in dev.	%-age that is in dev. (to nearest %)

Fürnberg-Morzin:

1:1	86	19	22
37:1	168	60	36
2:1	193	64	33
15:1	134	14	10
4:1	96	24	25
10:1	90	22	24
10:2	95	21	22
10:3	127	38	30
32:1	181	61	34
32:4	96	26	27
5:1	82	22	27

5:2......	134	 34	 25
11:1......	81	 23	 28
11:2......	163	 53	 33
33:1......	149	 51	 34
33:2......	105	 32	 30
27:1......	108	 26	 24
107:1......	113	 37	 33
107:2......	73	 23	 32
107:3......	72	 16	 22
3:1......	122	 34	 28
3:2......	86	 37	 43

Sturm und Drang:

39:1......	115	 31	 27
39:2......	100	 34	 34
39:4......	95	 32	 34
35:1......	177	 45	 25
35:2......	128	 36	 28
35:4......	141	 39	 28
59:1......	124	 29	 23
38:1......	194	 56	 29
38:2......	102	 38	 38
38:4......	153	 32	 21
49:1......	96	 18	 19
49:2......	140	 48	 34
49:4......	125	 36	 29
58:1......	195	 45	 23
26:1......	133	 35	 26
26:2......	80	 13	 16
41:1......	202	 53	 26
41:2......	89	 21	 24
41:4......	143	 25	 17
48:1......	196	 50	 26
48:2......	89	 19	 21
48:4......	160	 13	 8
44:1......	157	 39	 25
44:3......	83	 16	 20
44:4......	187	 44	 24

52:1.............. 163 ..... 44 27
52:2.............. 197 ..... 37 19
52:4.............. 188 ..... 58 31
43:1.............. 254 ..... 63 25
43:2.............. 120 ..... 32 27
43:4.............. 161 ..... 40 25
42:1.............. 224 ..... 51 23
42:2.............. 167 ..... 41 25
51:1.............. 209 ..... 67 32
51:2.............. 93 ..... 24 26
45:1.............. 209 ..... 69 33
45:2.............. 190 ..... 50 26
46:1.............. 141 ..... 45 30
46:2.............. 66 ..... 16 24
47:1.............. 159 ..... 57 36
47:4.............. 283 ..... 70 25
65:1.............. 129 ..... 8 6
65:2.............. 145 ..... 41 28
65:4.............. 84 ..... 21 25

London:

96:1.............. 203 ..... 70 34
95:1.............. 165 ..... 67 41
93:1.............. 262 ..... 74 28
94:1.............. 257 ..... 47 18
98:1.............. 320 ..... 77 24
98:2.............. 86 ..... 23 27
98:4.............. 386 ..... 84 22
97:1.............. 293 ..... 59 20
99:1.............. 202 ..... 48 24
99:2.............. 98 ..... 19 19
100:1.............. 289 ..... 85 29
101:1.............. 346 ..... 96 28
102:1.............. 311 ..... 117 38
103:1.............. 228 ..... 65 29
104:1.............. 294 ..... 69 23
104:4.............. 334 ..... 75 22

Average %-age of Full Sonata Form Movements
Comprised by Developments:

Fürnberg-Morzin........29%
<u>Sturm und Drang</u>........26%
London................27%

From the above table it appears that the <u>Sturm und Drang</u> symphonies are slightly less developmental than their Fürnberg-Morzin and London counterparts. In addition, the <u>Sturm und Drang</u> symphonies generally employ fewer tonal levels in their developments than the other symphonies examined in this chapter. This is especially so for the well-known minor-keyed works of the <u>Sturm und Drang</u>. It has also been remarked in this chapter that Haydn appears to be conservative in formal procedures when dealing with an unusual tonality and, vice versa, is harmonically adventurous in those movements pitched in familiar keys. The widely held belief that the <u>Sturm und Drang</u> symphonies are formally advanced (or at least unique among Haydn's orchestral compositions) must derive, in part, from the superficial display of a few unusual tonalities and the very natural human fallacy to equate increased length with increased complexity.

CHAPTER III

PROCESS

> Sometimes Apollo rouses his silent muse with his lyre and does not always bend his bow.
> -----Horace

Introduction: Haydn and his "Elementarbuch"

Haydn appears to have been very conscious of the various types of compositional processes by which musical forms can be realized. In the preceding chapter the range and complexity of Haydn's formal procedures were amply demonstrated and, therefore, it should not be at all surprising that a comparable diversity exists for the composer's selection of compositional processes.

Several factors from Haydn's early life and musical training may account for the conspicuously orthodox approach to composition that is revealed in his works. First of all, although Haydn received invaluable musical training from Georg Reutter (and to a lesser extent, Niccolo

Porpora), he was largely self-taught in composition.¹ The realization of the serious lacunae in his musical knowledge propelled Haydn to seek systematic instruction, pursuing what Geiringer has described as devouring "Johann Joseph Fux's famous <u>Gradus ad Parnassum</u>, Johann Mattheson's <u>Der vollkommene Kapellmeister</u>, and David Kellner's <u>Unterricht im Generalbass</u>."² Secondly, coupled with his desire for personal instruction, Haydn partly supported himself for a number of years by giving music lessons (which necessarily had to be pursued in a more or less systematic and orderly fashion). Haydn's personal instructional needs and his role as pedagogue interacted to a substantial degree, and there is a remarkably close affinity between his tenets as a teacher of composition and the manifestation of these tenets in his own compositions throughout his entire career. Nowhere is this phenomenon better or more specifically shown than by comparing the works with which this book is concerned with the principles of composition set forth in Haydn's <u>Elementarbuch</u>.³

---

¹In <u>Haydn: Chronicle and Works</u>, 1:60, Landon quotes the following from J. F. Rochlitz, <u>Für Freunde der Tonkunst</u>, Leipzig, 1832, 4:274:
    I [Haydn] never had real teachers. My beginning was always with the practical--first in singing and playing instruments, after that in composition.

²Geiringer, <u>Haydn: A Creative Life</u>, pp. 29-30.

³The <u>Elementarbuch</u> (or more specifically, <u>Elementarbuch der verschiednen Gattungen des Contrapuncts aus dem grösseren Wercken des Kappm. Fux, von Joseph Haydn zusammengezogen</u>) is a fragmentary discourse on the <u>Gradus ad Parnassum</u> of J. J. Fux either dictated to or copied by Haydn's composition student F. C. Magnus. The work is given in its original text with an English translation in Alfred Mann's article, "Haydn's Elementarbuch: A Document of Classic Counterpoint Instruction," <u>Music Forum</u> 3, pp. 197-237.

As would be expected of any good teacher of counterpoint, Haydn stresses the efficacy of contrary and oblique motions and advises the student to be wary of parallel motion.[4] Needless to say, contrary motion is most frequently found in Haydn's symphonic writing, too frequent indeed to cite specific examples. Substantial sections of oblique motion, however, are almost always presented as harbingers of syntactical alteration. In the earliest symphonies of Haydn, oblique motion almost always precedes false reprises. In the first movement of Symphony No. 37, the false reprise offers a way out of the G pedal (i.e., it effectively eliminates the tautological effect of the pedal). (See Symphony No. 37, movement one, mm. 69-82.) The second movement of Symphony No. 11 and the first movement of Symphony No. 33 also display this same phenomenon. (See Symphony No. 11, movement two, mm. 59-78 and Symphony No. 33, movement one, mm. 54-60.) In the fourth movement of Symphony No. 38 the quasi-false reprise (at measure 75) is closely linked with a C pedal. (See Symphony No. 38, movement four, mm. 67-80.)

Oblique motion also serves other compositional functions beside indicating syntactical alterations. In Symphony No. 18, movement two, a sonata form movement without development, oblique motion serves as an extension of expository material into the area in which the development would normally occur. (See Symphony No. 18, movement two, mm. 43-48.) In the third movement of Symphony No. 4 the A pedal serves as a condensation of developmental material, thereby masking the thematic tautologies in the upper strings and winds. (See Symphony No. 4, mm. 53-76.) At times, similar

---

[4]Ibid., p. 215.

instances of oblique motion may serve entirely different functions depending on their compositional position. In the first movement of Symphony No. 32 the G pedal (mm. 71-86) permits the delaying of the real development section; whereas, the G pedal of mm. 125-131 permits the anticipation of the recapitulation.

As Haydn proceeds into the Sturm und Drang and London symphonies, oblique motion becomes less associated as an introduction for the false reprise. In its place, however, are substituted the compositional devices of unison, solo, and silence. The following table indicates the remaining false reprises and how they are prepared.

TABLE 4

FALSE REPRISES AND THEIR PREPARATIONS

Symphony/movement	Preparation	False Reprise
Sturm und Drang:		
41:1	2 mm. of unison	m. 97
43:1	3 mm. of solo (VnI)	m. 105
42:1	silence	m. 89
51:1	silence	mm. 108-109 (wrong key)
46:1	solo (VnI)	m. 70
London:		
94:4	5 mm. of solo (VnI)	m. 146 (false reprise of tonality only)
97:1	6 mm. of sequence/ suspensions	m. 143

This discussion of the various types of motion and their relationship with abrupt changes of harmonic movement and compositional syntax reveals some interesting insights into the true nature of the role of "wit," or the so-called "typically Haydnesque" features of Haydn's orchestral writing (e.g., false reprises, deceptive cadences). If one considers the subconscious underpinnings of oblique and parallel motions (the two types of motion most often associated with preparations for abrupt syntactical shifts), it must be admitted that the preparatory material is as much or more unstable than the specific compositional device in which the change in syntax occurs. Oblique motion, by definition, is generally stable from an harmonic standpoint, and also tends to be very stable melodically, often acting as a framework for melodic tautologies that remain undeveloped. Passages featuring parallel motion may give a false sense of closure if they occur in the wrong syntactical position, thereby requiring a sudden change, the perfect example of which would be a false reprise. Therefore, the false reprise is, in reality, not the goal of a "typically Haydnesque wit" nor a feature of the simple charm of Haydn's dotage, but is a necessity of compositional logic in order to correct the false aural impressions given by earlier, unstable syntactical agents. In his early symphonies Haydn most often employed oblique motion to set the stage for the false reprise; later this changed to unisons, solos, or periods of silence. Consistently throughout his career, Haydn employed the false reprise not as an aural delight designed to confuse and amaze his listeners, but rather as compensation for previous periods of instability which were usually a rudimental form of oblique or contrary motion. Again, we see a sort of gyroscopic effect in Haydn's music; no matter how far the compositional symmetry becomes unbalanced, equilibrium almost always ensues.

In very specific and minute circumstances Haydn often displays a dazzling ability to alter in the subtlest manner the type of motion he is employing. At times Haydn avoids parallel motion by taking recourse to oblique motion which involves only the inclusion of a stationary note. As an example of this, see Symphony No. 45, movement one, measures 102-107. In the example just mentioned, oblique motion is coupled with syncopation in order to avoid parallel motion. Again, as has been seen so often in connection with musical phenomena such as the false reprise, oblique motion acts as a preparation for a syntactical agent, this time being a period of silence. Haydn's practice here is wholly consistent with his pedagogical dictates. In commenting about 1st species counterpoint he presents the following caveat:

> NB. In this species [1st] of counterpoint one should avoid using many unisons or octaves. They yield too little variety of sound. Excepted are the beginning and end of a piece, where they can be more easily accepted.[5]

The use of oblique motion as a harbinger of syntactical change is very consistent throughout the course of Haydn's artistic career. In Symphony No. 101, movement one, measures 31-48, Haydn goes through all three types of motion in rapid succession before settling on oblique, which then serves as the preparation for the agent of syntactical alteration (in this case, a unison between Flute I and Violin I). (Measures 33-40 contain contrary motion;

---

[5]Mann, "Haydn's Elementarbuch," p. 223.

measures 41-42 parallel motion; measures 43-44 contrary motion; and measures 45-48 oblique motion.)

Another interesting example of Haydn's compositional procedures closely adhering to the principles set forward in the <u>Elementarbuch</u> is the composer's advice that "one should give particular attention in this species [2nd] of composition not to connect two successive fifths or octaves by the <u>skip of a third</u>, which is not permissible...."[6] Haydn faced such a problem at the beginning of both movements two and three in his Symphony No. 39. In movement two the intervals are arranged so that the successive fifths occur only on beats two and three, relatively weak beats in 3/8 meter. (See Symphony No. 39, movement two, mm. 1-3.) This procedure is in perfect accord with Haydn's dictum that:

> ...it will always be better to consider the end ahead of time. In order to make this species [2nd] easier one may use a half rest in place of a <u>first note</u> occurring on the thesis.[7]

Although the musical examples from the <u>Gradus</u> to which Haydn was referring are in duple meter, the principle functions nicely in the above example in triple meter. Obviously, Haydn did not conceive of composition as a strictly linear process, but more as a <u>Gestalt</u> in which all points of reference were created at approximately the same time and in which an alteration of one point perforce impinged upon all the other points. In movement three the displacement of the viola/cello line was now coupled with contrary motion in the upper strings. (See Symphony No. 39, movement

---

[6]Ibid., p. 229.

[7]Ibid., p. 227.

three, mm. 1-3.)

Species Counterpoint

Fuxian counterpoint dominated much of Haydn's contrapuntal thinking and practice. As will be demonstrated later in this chapter, species counterpoint, as the point of departure with respect to compositional processes, appears approximately evenly in all three groups of symphonies with which this book is concerned. It seems almost axiomatic to state that of the five species the first, second, and third (i.e., respectively, note against note, two notes to one, and four [or three] notes to one) are employed an overwhelmingly large proportion of the time.

Fourth species counterpoint (i.e., the use of suspensions) appears deliberately and at regular intervals in Haydn's music. It is the conspicuous presence of fourth species counterpoint, along with Haydn's well-known admiration of the Gradus as a pedagogical tool, that confirms the appropriateness of utilizing species counterpoint as a vehicle for analysis. All composers of the classic era, whether by volition or by accident, employed 1st, 2nd, and 3rd species in their compositions. The regularity of 4th species counterpoint in Haydn's music, a phenomenon that could hardly be construed as accidental, tends to confirm the degree to which Fuxian counterpoint preoccupied the compositional thinking of Haydn.

Fifth species counterpoint, or florid counterpoint, is the least specific of the five Fuxian classifications. The author of the Gradus himself states:

As a garden is full of flowers so this species of counterpoint

[5th] should be full of excellences of all kinds, a plastic melody line, liveliness of movement, and beauty and variety of form. Just as we use all the other common species of arithmetic--counting, addition, multiplication and subtraction--in division, so this species is nothing but a recapitulation and combination of all the preceding ones.[8]

In instances of 5th species counterpoint the various component compositional processes will be indicated.

Sequencing and Other Compositional Processes

Sequencing plays a large role in the selection of Haydn's compositional processes. Unlike the baroque sequence (in which the process was generally a means of simply moving from one tonal level to another), Haydn's sequences fulfill many functions and are quite varied in design and purpose. At times sequences will appear as the agents whereby thematic material is presented, only to have implicit tonal goals remain unfulfilled, or at least in opposition to those goals implied by the tonal dictates of the form in which they are present. For this and other reasons that will become clearer as this chapter continues, three specific types of sequences are enumerated and named. (1) <u>Figurative Sequence</u>--This type of sequence has at least three occurrences of the sequential pattern, conforming in both tonal progression

---

[8]Alfred Mann, trans. and ed., <u>The Study of Counterpoint from Johann Joseph Fux's "Gradus ad Parnassum"</u>, rev. ed. (New York: W.W. Norton, 1971), p. 64.

and rhythmic/intervallic configuration. An example of a figurative sequence is as follows:

(2) <u>Tonal Sequence</u>-- In this type of sequence the tonal goal is reached at the beginning of what would be the third sequential statement while the rhythmic/intervallic figuration breaks down at the same point. Several examples of tonal sequences are:

(3) <u>Abortive Sequence</u>-- This final type of sequence is that in which the tonal goal is not reached at what would be the third sequential statement; rather, the sequence is abandoned. An example of an abortive sequence is:

Another factor determining the importance of sequences is that very often they are coupled with instances of 4th species counterpoint.

Several compositional processes that are very often used as agents or harbingers of syntactical alteration will be given special attention in the ensuing pages of this chapter. These include periods of silence, solos, and unisons. All three processes have already been given some attention in their relationships with specific types of motion; however, their functioning is more complicated and the number of times they occur is much greater than has already been indicated. Silence is a particularly interesting compositional device and requires our attention in that it is often regarded as one of the "unique" features of the Sturm und Drang. Solos and unisons are regarded as naive processes, seemingly more in the province of orchestration than composition itself; however, their importance in musical semiotics belies their unsophisticated façade. The approach and methodology for the analysis of solos and unisons (and by extension, to periods of silence) utilizes certain aspects of a theoretical model proposed by Janet M. Levy concerning texture as a semiotic agent.[9]

Other compositional processes to be discussed in the following pages will include the various types of variations, fugue, fugato, canons, inversions, and retrograde movement.

Thematic Development and Transformation

---

[9]Janet M. Levy, "Texture as a Sign in Classic and Early Romantic Music," Journal of the American Musicological Society 35 (1982): 482-531. In this article Levy identifies accompanimental devices (such as the Alberti bass) in addition to solos and unisons as musico-semiotic devices. The author of the present study has chosen to omit such accompanimental devices as they are more typical of keyboard music than the symphonic genre.

Theoretical discussions of Haydn's manner of composition seem to be preoccupied with thematic or motivic development. Haydn, more so than either Mozart or Beethoven, is regarded as the avatar of thematic development, supposedly lacking the melodic gift of Mozart and the trail-blazing originality and profundity of Beethoven. Several important reasons contribute to this perception. (1) Haydn employed imitative processes (e.g., fugue, fugato, canon, and canonic-like writing) in a fairly prevalent and consistent manner throughout his lifetime. In an imitative musical form the entire structure is implicit in the theme, as much so as a form of life is implicit in its monocellular state. From a musical standpoint, if the biological analogy is continued, it would appear that the entire musical structure is the inevitable consequence of the theme itself and not the compositional processes involved. (2) Haydn's music is overwhelmingly perceived to be generally monothematic, thereby making the "development" of the single theme a compositional necessity since there are no possibilities for dramatic tension via the juxtaposition of opposing themes; the overestimation of Haydn's monothematicism, however, does not hold up to close scrutiny. Charles Rosen speaks very persuasively on this subject:

> By the late 1780s most composers used a new theme at the arrival of the dominant (and many already used another theme to initiate the modulation to the dominant as well): Haydn's procedure [repetition of tonic theme at the dominant level] was flagrantly eccentric to general practice, and was remarked as such....[T]he Mercure de France praised 'this vast genius, who in each one of his pieces knows how to draw developments so rich and varied from a unique theme (sujet)-- very different from those sterile composers who shift continually from one idea to another for lack of knowing how to present one idea in varied forms....' This is the origin of the myth of Haydn's so-called monothematicism--a myth because every one

of these movements contains several themes, even if a new theme is not always used to confirm the new key in the exposition.[10]

While effectively negating the argument for emphasis upon thematic development due to monothematicism, Rosen later emphasizes thematic considerations on account of polythematicism:

> If we wish today to describe the late eighteenth-century form [sonata form] which could be realized in such different ways by Haydn and by his contemporaries, then it will clearly not do to use the number and position of the themes as defining characteristics; nor, on the other hand, will it be reasonable to dismiss the thematic structure as merely a surface manifestation of a deeper harmonic structure (although this too has been proposed in our time); the themes and their order clearly had an important role to play.[11]

While not denying the importance of thematic considerations, it is clear from the quotation above that Rosen perceives sonata form in terms of harmonic and thematic outlines; nowhere is mention made of the various compositional processes by which the individuality of a composer was so commonly expressed. Indeed, what is a theme if not the catalyst and carrier of a compositional process? This chapter, therefore, is an attempt to redress the exclusion of process from theoretical discussions of eighteenth-century music in general and Haydn's compositions in particular.

Another reason for emphasizing the role of compositional processes

---

[10] Charles Rosen, Sonata Forms (New York: W.W. Norton, 1980), p. 5.

[11] Ibid.

rather than thematic or motivic development is the undue attention given to the idea of a theme or motive acquiring organic properties. Organicism is very much a concept of the nineteenth century, a time in which theoreticians of the arts found themselves influenced to a great extent by scientific concepts, particularly the Darwinian theory of evolution. This preoccupation with an organic, evolutionary theoretical foundation for the composition of music has affected much of the thinking of musicologists and music theorists down to the present day. Witness the following quotation from Rudolph Reti's The Thematic Process in Music:

> In a sonata or symphony, on the contrary, the spirit of the form is fulfilled only if the shapes are transformed in such a way that the new theme seems to be entirely different from the one from which it is derived. True, Haydn in his symphonies sometimes introduces a theme that according to all signs of the outer proportions represents a second theme but proves to be a mere repetition of the first theme. In the light of the ensuing evolution, however, this must be considered a problematic shaping--a shaping that may be explained simply by the fact that in this early stage the deeper idea of the symphonic form and the thematic technique through which it was expressed were not fully realized even by the same great musical mind who, in a sense, must be regarded as its father and discoverer. But in the advanced symphonic style, the era of genuine thematic transformation, a composer's ability to form a theme from a preceding one must be considered the more effective, the less the outer similarity of the two themes is recognizable, in spite of the identity of the kernel.[12]

The above quotation is of particular importance because it stresses that

---

[12]Rudolph Reti, The Thematic Process in Music (New York: The Macmillan Co., 1951), pp. 57-58.

monothematicism and organic thematic development are linked in the minds of those who favor an evolutionary model for musical composition.

Reti's position is supported by Jan LaRue who asserts very confidently that Haydn employed a technique (which LaRue styles as multistage variance) in which all thematic material is ultimately derived from an U̱r-theme or motive, the succeeding themes or subthemes being very small incremental variations (or variations of variations and so forth) of the original theme.[13] LaRue presents a highly detailed analysis of some of Haydn's works and wisely tries to distance himself from the matter of monothematicism, stating that the term "does not adequately describe this technique, since it suggests limitation, the very opposite of the sense of boundless variety one experiences in the continual unfolding of Haydn's ideas."[14] This shunning of the term monothematicism, however, is very superficial because central to the very concept of multistage variance is the idea of the unifying, organic single theme. In addition, stating that one musical theme, motive, or cell is derived from another (due to supposed similarities of pitch, rhythm, or general linear direction, which may or may not be accidental) is largely a matter of highly subjective interpretation. On the other hand, multistage variance cannot be conclusively disproved in that there is much circumstantial evidence in its support.

There are, however, equally powerful arguments against the theory that a similarity among thematic material is an indication of "thematic

---

[13] Jan LaRue, "Multistage Variance: Haydn's Legacy to Beethoven," The Journal of Musicology 1 (1982): 265-274.

[14] Ibid., p. 265.

development" or "thematic mutation (or transformation or metamorphosis)." Leonard Ratner has suggested that so-called melodic permutations are the result of the influence of the ars combinatoria practices of the seventeenth and eighteenth centuries.[15] By this line of reasoning "thematic development" is really a matter of the interchangeability of motives rather than an evolution from one motive into another.

Interestingly enough, Heinrich Schenker, while affirming the essentially biological nature of the motif, views thematic material in a non-evolutionary manner:

#6. The Biological Nature of Form

> Also within the above-mentioned larger formal units [sonata and lied forms], the biological momentum of music recurs in an amazing way. For what is the fundamental purpose of the turns and tricks of the cyclical form? To represent the destiny, the real personal fate of a motif or of several motifs simultaneously. The sonata represents the motifs in ever changing situations in which their characters are revealed, just as human beings are represented in a drama.
>
> For this is just what happens in a drama: men are led through situations in which their characters are tested in all their shades and grades, so that one characteristic feature is revealed in each particular situation. And what is character as a whole, if not a synthesis of these qualities which have been revealed by such a sequence of situations?
>
> The life of a motif is represented in an analogous way. The motif is led through various situations. At one time, its melodic character is tested; at another time, a harmonic peculiarity must prove its valor in unaccustomed surroundings; a third time, again, the motif is subjected to some rhythmic change: in other words, the motif lives through its fate, like a personage in a drama.

---

[15]Ratner, Classic Music, pp. 98-102.

> Obviously, these destinies, in drama as well as in music, are, so to speak, quantitatively reduced and stylized according to the law of abbreviation. Thus it would be of no interest at all to see Wallenstein having lunch on the stage regularly during the whole process of dramatic development. For everyone knows that he must have lunched daily; and the poet could therefore omit the dramatic presentation of these quite unessential lunches in order to concentrate the drama on the essential moments of his hero's life. In an analogous way the composer applies the law of abbreviation to the destiny of the motif, the hero of his drama. From the infinity of situations into which his motif could conceivably fall, he must choose a few. These, however, must be so chosen that the motif is forced to reveal in them its character in all its aspects and peculiarities.
>
> Thus it is illicit, according to the law of abbreviation, to present the motif in a situation which cannot contribute anything new to the clarification of its character. No composer could hope to reveal through overloaded, complicated, and unessential matter what could be revealed by a few, but well-chosen, fatal moments in the life of a motif. It will be of no interest at all to hear how the motif, metaphorically speaking, makes its regular evening toilet, takes its regular lunch, etc.[16]

Given the highly original theories of Schenker regarding harmonic analysis and his emphasis on the linear aspects of music, it should not be too surprising that he places great importance on the compositional processes of a work of music (which are realized linearally) while viewing thematic material as essentially static by both design and necessity. This is, in reality, the first suggestion, albeit veiled, that in an explanation of the inner workings of a musical composition the compositional processes are of more importance than the theme itself.

---

[16]Heinrich Schenker, Harmony, ed. by Oswald Jonas, trans. by Elizabeth Mann Borgese (Chicago: University of Chicago Press, 1954), pp. 12-13.

Pursuing in a completely different manner the question of the primacy of compositional processes vs. thematic development, Arnold Salop, in a particularly trenchant essay entitled "Intensity and the Classical Sonata Allegro,"[17] suggested that occurrences of redundant musical material (i.e., repetitions of themes or thematic material) happen an overwhelmingly large percentage of the time during periods of low harmonic/rhythmic/dramatic intensity.[18] Salop states that in order to present redundant material effectively "such powerful effects as a change of key, a strong cadence, or a forceful presentation of important thematic material should be avoided."[19] The implication of Salop's reasoning is that a lack of harmonic modulation is a prerequisite for the presentation of redundant melodic material or, in other words, that the harmonic outline of a composition (which to the classic style is the sine qua non of form) determines the shape of so-called thematic development.

Related tangentially to Salop's theory is the idea of Charles Rosen's that in the classic style the musical forms are distinguished by a series of key centers, tonal "peaks" as it were, which require the composer to "fill in" the areas between these "peaks":

> ...[T]he classical style needed more forceful means of emphasizing new keys than the Baroque, and it used for this purpose a quantity of 'filling' almost unparalleled until then in

---

[17]Arnold Salop, "Intensity and the Classical Sonata Allegro," in <u>Studies in the History of Musical Style</u> (Detroit: Wayne State University Press, 1971), pp. 215-249.

[18]Ibid., pp. 230-231.

[19]Ibid., p. 231.

the history of music except in pieces of an improvisatory character. By 'filling' I mean purely conventional material, superficially unrelated to the content of the piece, and apparently (and in some cases, actually) transferable bodily from one work to another. Every musical style, naturally, relies on conventional material, principally at cadences, which almost always follow traditional formulas. The classical style, however, further magnified and elongated the cadence in order to strengthen the modulation. A Baroque composer worked mostly with vertical filling (the figured bass), and the classical composer with horizontal: long phrases of conventional passagework. Aside from accompaniment figures and cadential ornaments, the two basic forms of conventional material are scales and arpeggios, and they fill classical works to a degree that would only have been possible for a Baroque composer in a toccata, or in a form that tried to sound improvised rather than composed. The means employed by an early eighteenth-century composer to give the impression of freedom were needed by Mozart to organize the form; he used whole phrases of scales and arpeggios the way Handel used sequences--to tie sections of the work together. But in the finest Baroque work the sequence is generally clothed and covered by thematic material, while even in the greatest works of Haydn and Mozart the 'filling' is displayed nakedly and appears to have been prefabricated in large pieces.[20]

What Rosen appears to be suggesting is that there is in classic music a hierarchy of phenomena (listed here in descending order of importance):

    (1) archetypal harmonic outlines
    (2) conventionalized compositional processes
    (3) thematic material

The juxtaposition of thematic material and compositional processes would

---

[20]Charles Rosen, The Classical Style, p. 71.

tend to give the impression that the thematic material was being "developed," even tough there may have been no conceptual linkage between the two envisioned by the composer.

The line of reasoning presented in this section of the chapter demonstrates that the conflict between thematic development and compositional processes is hardly resolved. Quite surprisingly, little formal analysis of the compositional processes employed in groups of musical works has been attempted to date. This serves, in no little part, to justify this chapter's emphasis on the processes utilized by Haydn in his Fürnberg-Morzin, <u>Sturm und Drang</u>, and London symphonies rather than identifying the themes and motives of the same works and charting them through an evolutionary course.

Musical compositions typically begin and end with some degree of closure. Musical analysis, however, is of a more cyclic nature, with ideas and approaches of seemingly disparate nature constantly reappearing and interacting with one another to a very substantial degree. In the following quotation, Carl Dahlhaus effects a "recapitulation" of sorts, seeing in the idea of the organic theme a close connection with the <u>Zeitgeist</u>:

> ...[M]usic histories were once conceived primarily in terms of composers, forms, genres and even nations.... Music historians drew on three patently incongruous axioms as though they were self-evident truths: (1) that outstanding composers 'make' music history...; (2) that musical genres evolve in the same way as natural organisms (as though music history were part of natural history); and (3) that this evolution in the musical culture of a nation expresses and embodies its 'national spirit' (as though north and south Germany shared a common 'national' music

history).[21]

Put another way, Dahlhaus sees the effort to explain musical and thematic "evolution" as an organic process as being directly connected with the attempt to interpret music history as an expression of the Zeitgeist. By this manner of reasoning, musical "organisms" (forms, themes, motives) are direct manifestations of the Zeitgeist. The link between the evolutionary approach to musical analysis and the Zeitgeist is significant because (as already seen in this chapter and in Chapter I) both have contributed to the layers of assumptions surrounding the compositions contained within the Sturm und Drang label, namely, that the Sturm und Drang style is a self-contained category existing within a continually evolving formal framework and that the musical Sturm und Drang is the objectification of the European Zeitgeist of the 1770s.

Fürnberg-Morzin Symphonies

The first symphony of the Fürnberg-Morzin group, No 1. in D major is of particular interest historically because it represents Haydn's initial thoughts regarding the types of compositional processes to be employed in the symphonic genre. With the singular exception of solos, nearly every type of compositional process is encountered in the course of this work that the composer would utilize throughout his entire career: unison, 1st, 2nd, and 3rd species counterpoint, sequences, and imitative writing. In movement one

---

[21]Dahlhaus, Foundations of Music History, p. 131.

several interesting features make their first appearance and will become standard features of Haydn's later works. The first is the use of imitation, not only between two single lines, but between pairs of instrumental lines. (See Symphony No. 1, movement 1, mm. 76-77.) Haydn will steadily increase the complexity of this device, with greater independence developing between the individual members of each pair and, especially in the London symphonies, more doubling by the winds and brasses. The second compositional device first appearing in this movement is the use of a sequence pattern and/or a chain of suspensions to precede the point of furthest remove (vi, at measure 55). (See Symphony No. 1, movement one, mm. 47-55.)

The following table lists from the remaining symphonies included in this study those movements in sonata form with discernible points of furthest remove and the processes by which they are approached.

TABLE 5

COMPOSITIONAL PROCESSES UTILIZED TO APPROACH
POINTS OF FURTHEST REMOVE

Sym./mvt.	m. of PFR	Process(es)	mm. of Process(es)
Fürnberg-Morzin:			
37:1	101	sequence	96-100
2:1	86	sequence over pedal	83-85
15:1	73	sequence	69
15:3	36	sequence	34-36
4:1	51	suspensions	50-52

10:2	53	sequence	48-54
32:1	97	1st, 2nd, 3rd [species]	entire mvt
32:4	48	sequence	39-50
5:2	69	sequence/suspensions	66-68
11:2	86	sequence	81-86
11:4	59	suspensions/sequence	55-62
33:1	72	sequence/imitation	72-77
27:1	57	abortive sequence	57-61
3:1	72	sequence/suspensions	66-68

Sturm und Drang:

39:2	54	1st, 2nd, 3rd	ca. all mvt
35:1	95	sequence	88-94
35:2	76	unison	76-80
59:1	67	sequence/imitation	57-61
38:1	95	syncopation	76-93
38:2	47	1st, hocketing	ca. all mvt
58:1	73	1st, 2nd, 3rd	73ff
41:1	126	sequence	111-119
41:4	79	unison	75-78
48:1	110	sequence	103-109
52:2	98	unison	96-97
43:1	105	tonal sequence	101-105
43:2	59	sequence/suspensions	53-58
43:4	79	solo (Violin I)	74-76
42:1	88	silence	88
42:2	93	sequence/suspensions	85-90
51:1	107	silence	107
45:2	110	1st, 2nd, 3rd	110ff
46:1	66	imitation	60-65
46:4	72	silence	70-71
47:1	61	sequence	57-68
47:4	124	1st, 2nd, 3rd	124ff
65:1	54	1st, 2nd, 3rd	54ff

London:

96:1	86	1st, 2nd, 3rd	86ff
93:1	136	sequence	122-127
94:1	148	1st, 2nd, 3rd	148ff

98:1	191	1st, 2nd, 3rd	191ff
98:2	46	1st, 2nd, 3rd	46ff
99:1	94	silence	93
99:2	52	abortive sequence	47-50
100:1	170	1st, 2nd, 3rd	170ff
103:1	108	sequence/suspensions	105-107
104:1	179	1st, 2nd, 3rd	179ff
104:4	139	1st, 2nd, 3rd	139ff

As can be seen in the table above, Haydn is amazingly consistent in all three periods of symphonic composition in his utilization of specific compositional processes for numerous specific compositional events, particularly the point of furthest remove and its approach.

The second and third movements of Symphony No. 1, on the other hand, are both sonata forms without developments and are quite simple in terms of formal (i.e., tonal) construction. However, for their size both movements employ a large number of compositional processes (such as unisons, sequences, and suspensions) in order to serve as generative forces acting in lieu of the more sustained tonal development that is characteristic of the full sonata form. This is the first instance of what may be considered a lifelong stylistic trait or eccentricity of Haydn's, namely, that a simple formal outline is _generally_ balanced by the occurrence of a number of compositional processes (imitation, sequences, suspensions, and syncopation) which serve as the motivating forces of the movement, replacing the forward impetus generated by a series of modulations. For the sake of convenience, we will refer to this tendency as the simple formal/complex process theorem.

This simple formal/complex process theorem is well supported by a perusal of Symphony No. 37 in C major, the next work chronologically in the Fürnberg-Morzin series. The first movement has a development that establishes only the submediant level in addition to the tonic and dominant, yet almost every conceivable type of compositional process is employed: suspension, sequence, unisons, imitation, and all of the various contrapuntal species including the 5th. (See Symphony No. 37, movement one, mm. 127-134 for an example of 5th species counterpoint.) The second movement minuet and trio employs a number of processes (besides species 1-3), each being utilized only once throughout the course of the movement. Of particular interest is the way in which Haydn subtly alters his processes. Invertible counterpoint is displayed in a strict manner (Symphony No. 37, movement two, mm. 25-30), and then is employed in a less restrictive fashion (Symphony No 37, movement two, mm. 33-35). The generative impetus of the third movement is accomplished through the use of two sequence patterns. The first (Symphony No. 37, movement three, mm. 10-13) is in an ascending pattern and occurs in the exposition; the second (Symphony No. 37, movement three, mm. 35-37) occurs in the development, and, in keeping with the classical ideal of symmetry, proceeds in a descending pattern.

The simple formal/complex process theorem holds true as well for the next Fürnberg-Morzin work, Symphony No. 18 in G major. Symphony No. 18 is even simpler in terms of form than the previous work, with its three movements consisting (in order) of two sonata forms without developments and a minuet and trio. The first movement begins with canonic activity at the interval of the 4th between the 2nd and 1st violins. (See Symphony No. 18, movement one, mm. 1-7.) The idea of the canon later becomes strict in its presentation, first at measures 30-36, and then at measures 45-49. The significance of the two passages mentioned in the previous sentence is that they help us to illustrate a point that will be seen very often in later symphonies, namely, that Haydn often presents a compositional process (not a thematic idea) in an incomplete or "impure" state at or near the beginning of a movement which later finds fulfillment in a more complete state at the middle or end of the same movement. It is the idea of the compositional process, not the thematic or motivic idea, that is transformed, altered, or even transmogrified. Although the melodies of the examples from Symphony No. 18, movement one are similar, many pairs of examples in the ensuing pages of this chapter will display little or no thematic resemblances.

Movements two and three of Symphony No. 18 contain Haydn's first use of tonal and abortive sequences in a symphonic setting. In movement three, the tonal sequence occurs at measures 9-13; the abortive sequence is found at measures 51-54. In later symphonies, particularly those of the London period, the abortive will generally appear first and then will seek resolution in tonal and/or figurative sequences. The importance of Symphony No. 18 is difficult to discern except in relation to Haydn's overall development as a symphonic composer. However, it is clear from an analysis of the aforementioned information that Haydn was pursuing (if not consciously, then at least at a subconscious level) the detachment of the development or fulfillment of implicit musical goals of the various compositional processes from the idea of thematic or motivic development.

In the next work of this series, Symphony No. 2 in C major, Haydn abandons the approach that was taken in the previous two symphonies, and this time successfully unites complex formal schema with a wide array of compositional processes. The first movement of this work has a development employing many tonal levels coupled with virtually every type of eighteenth-century compositional process, yielding a veritable compendium of species counterpoint. Haydn displays a greater forcefulness than has been previously seen in his use of various semiotic devices, such as the point of silence that serves as an abrupt line of demarcation between the pianissimo end of the development and the fortissimo beginning of the recapitulation (at measure 133).[22] This overtly dramatic device is generally seen as a stylistic feature of the composer's later symphonies. The second movement is basically durchcomponiert, with the forward impetus provided not by the display of any compositional process in particular, but by the almost complete absence of 1st species counterpoint. The first and second movements of this work provide an interesting contrast: the first driven by incessant modulations and ever-changing compositional processes, and the second by an equivalent lack in both categories. The third movement is Haydn's first attempt at a symphonic rondo and is characterized by a preoccupation with imitative processes; the bulk of the movement's linear impetus is the result of the compartmentalized tonal organization of the rondo form itself.

Symphony No. 15 in D major is in many ways a summation of the various compositional processes in the works mentioned above. This work is distinguished by its adagio introduction and finale, both of which employ a type of "hocketing" device in the accompanying instruments. (See Symphony

---

[22]William E. Grim, "A New Look at the Sturm und Drang: A Comparative Analysis of Haydn's Symphonies Nos. 2, 45 ('Farewell'), and 73 ('La Chasse')," paper presented at the Fall meeting of the Southeast Chapter of the American Musicological Society at Virginia Polytechnic Institute on October 1, 1983.

No. 15, movement one, mm. 1-4.) The remainder of this movement is motivated by a wide array of additional compositional processes. The second movement minuet and trio employs a larger number of compositional processes than are normally seen in movements of this type. Of special significance is Haydn's manner in which the illusion of imitation is given (particularly paired imitation) by the alteration of sections of solo instruments with the violin section. (See Symphony No. 15, movement two, mm. 33-46.) The illusion of imitation, therefore, is accomplished via orchestration. The third movement is motivated by a tonal sequence (except in Violin I in which case the sequence is figurative). (See Symphony No. 15, movement three, mm. 16-18.) Later , this sequence is realized figuratively in all four parts. (See Symphony No. 15, movement three, mm. 34-36.) Finally, the fourth movement, which is a hybrid of ternary and rondo forms, finds its "minore" section given its generative thrust by the inclusion of one sequence pattern. (See Symphony No. 15, movement four, mm. 83-88.) As has been seen already in the case of the finale of Symphony No. 2, movements utilizing the rondo generally have recourse to few specific types of compositional processes given the usually short and sectionalized nature of the harmonic outline. Only in the "minore" section of the final movement of Symphony No. 15 was it necessary to employ a compositional process other than a rather basic type of 1st, 2nd, or 3rd species counterpoint. By definition, the middle minor section needed only to go back to the tonic, whereas, the outlying major sections had much more specific and direct harmonic goals. In many of the works to follow, Haydn will display great skill in generating a short movement (rondos, minuets and trios--even some sonata forms) by employing only one sequence pattern.

Symphony No. 4 in D major is closely connected to its predecessor by way of the similarity and scope of the compositional processes of both works. Movement one makes conspicuous use of a type of paired imitation which, while hardly strict in nature, is nevertheless a fulfillment of the false imitation that was the main feature of the trio of the second movement of Symphony No. 15. (See Symphony No. 4, movement one, mm. 23-31.) The idea of deceiving the listener, so effective a device in Symphony No. 15, is employed in two different cases in the third movement of Symphony No. 4. The first instance is a type of false canon at the interval of the 5th that is effected between the 1st and 2nd violins which quickly breaks down into homophony. (See Symphony No. 4, movement four, mm. 12-15.) The second instance is the entire development section (measures 53-76) which never really develops in that a pedal point on A is constantly repeated throughout the section. The second movement has already been discussed in detail in Chapter I and is notable for its continuous syncopation and durchcomponiert construction. Once again, Haydn is deceiving the listener by providing no relief to the incessant chain of syncopation and suspensions.

Symphony No. 10 in D major lends some support to the simple formal/complex process theorem elaborated above. Only the tonic and dominant tonal levels figure prominently in the first movement, yet a very sophisticated assortment of compositional processes is presented, particularly in combination. One interesting example is found in measures 24-29 in which a quasi-imitative texture is superimposed on what is basically 5th species counterpoint. (In addition, measures 24-25 contain solo passages for the violins.) This procedure is repeated in the recapitulation. The development, on the other hand, is motivated by an abortive sequence, one of the clearest and most ostentatious occurrences of this device seen so far in this book. (See Symphony No. 10, movement one, mm. 51-53.) The second movement is similarly conceived as the first, with its exposition and recapitulation punctuated by a series of solo passages in the violins while its development is given impetus almost exclusively by a rather lengthy sequential passage (mm. 48-54). The idea of the sequence, found in the abortive form in the development of the first movement, is finally brought to fruition in the development of the second movement in which it appears in its complete figurative form. The third movement of Symphony No. 10 is notable here only for the short chain of sequences and suspensions in its development (mm. 68-76). Therefore, the idea of the sequence has found three manifestations of increasing complexity in this symphony: the abortive form in the first movement; the figurative form in the second movement; and finally, in the third movement, the figurative form linked with suspensions.

Symphonies No. 32 in C major and No. 5 in A major represent a significant decrease in the complexity of compositional processes from those encountered in the previous two symphonies. The most notable features of Symphony No. 5 include an imitative presentation in the two violin parts in the trio of movement three, and a finale (a sonata form without development) whose sole motivating force is a series of suspensions (mm. 1-4, 7-10, 12-15, 20-22, 27-31, 34-39, 44-47). These suspensions occur no less than seven times in a movement whose total length is only fifty nine measures. This is another instance in which Haydn comfortably sustains a short movement with only one main compositional idea.

Symphony No. 11 in Eb major provides an interesting contrast to works such as Symphonies Nos. 2 and 10 in which there are wide differences in the

99

number and scope of compositional processes between the various movements of each work. This is not the case with Symphony No. 11. Each movement of this work contains an approximately equally complex harmonic scheme (3 to 4 tonal levels) and similarly, an approximately equally complex set of compositional processes. Each movement, however, appears to concentrate on one compositional process in particular: movement one with imitation; movement two with long sequences and suspensions; movement three with suspensions (via syncopation); and movement four with short sequences and suspensions.[23]

An interesting phenomenon found in movement one is an abortive sequence which takes place immediately after the recapitulation. (See Symphony No. 11, movement one, mm. 58-60. The fulfillment of this abortive sequence, however, does not occur until the development of movement two. (See Symphony No. 11, movement two, mm. 90-95.) There are similarities of both pitch and motion at the beginnings of these two examples. Although a convincing argument could be made for this figurative resolution of an abortive sequence being the result of mere coincidence, a couple of points should be kept in mind. (1) The abortive sequence occurs at a very unusual position in the first movement, embellishing the recapitulation, but in reality, it is not a necessary feature of the recapitulation. It is almost as though

---

[23]An interesting sidelight to Symphony No. 11 is that it is one of only four works (the others being Symphonies Nos. 18, 5, and 49) of the forty four covered in this book which have the same key for all movements. This similarity of formal and process complexities among movements in a symphony having the same key for all movements suggests that there may be a connection between tonality and process, not unlike that of tonality and aesthetic perception. This hypothesis, however, is beyond the scope of this book but remains a tantalizing prospect for future research.

Haydn were meaning for the listener to keep this late feature of the first movement in mind. (2) Time and again, Haydn has demonstrated a capacity to link not only the movements of one work through similar themes and/or formal schema, but also groups (especially pairs) of symphonies. That a process begun in one movement would be fulfilled or resolved in a later movement does not seem to be out of keeping with the composer's idiosyncratic manner of composing as revealed so far in this study.

Haydn's next symphony, No. 33 in C major, is very different from its predecessor. The first movement is another example of a C major sonata form movement with a harmonically complex development which employs only a modicum of different types of compositional processes. The chief motivating force of this movement is a sequence pattern which occurs once in the exposition, development, and recapitulation (mm. 20-24, 72-77, and 118-122). Of the remaining three movements, the second contains one sequence pattern (mm. 66-68), the third movement one chain of suspensions (mm. 27-34), while the final movement, with a less harmonically complex formal scheme than the initial movement, displays a concomitant wider array of compositional processes (unison, sequence, suspensions, and imitation).

Symphony No. 27 in G major forms with its predecessor another one of those compositional pairs of which so much attention has already been paid. The second movement of this work is a very short sonata form which is almost entirely given over to second species counterpoint. The sole motivating force of the development section is a short sequence (mm. 25-27). The idea of the single compositional process giving the forward thrust to a short movement, therefore, links this movement with the second and third movement of Symphony No. 33 (see above).

A more interesting phenomenon from Symphony No. 27 occurs in its first movement where a highly sophisticated procedure is employed by Haydn with regard to the abortive sequence and its fulfillment. Two abortive sequences appear in close proximity in the development section (mm. 48-54 and 57-60). The fulfillment of the sequential idea occurs in the recapitulation (at mm. 85-89).

The final figurative sequence closely resembles the abortive sequence at measures 57-60 due to the descending motion of the cello/bass line and the similarities of the upper voices in both examples. The abortive sequence at measures 48-54, with its ascending direction, acts as an antecedent phrase to its successor at measures 57-60.

Symphony No. 107 in Eb major is somewhat unusual in that all of its movements are sonata forms with developments. The three movements, however, are roughly equivalent in terms of formal complexity and have a commensurate similarity in terms of the degree of complexity of compositional processes. The first movement emphasizes sequences or sequences allied with another process; the second movement almost exclusively features 1st and 2nd species counterpoint; while the third movement employs very short sequential passages.

The final work of the Fürnberg-Morzin group, Symphony No. 3 in G major is notable for one compositional process, namely, the fugue that is grafted onto the sonata form of its final movement. It has already been remarked in Chapter II that Symphony No. 3 holds a unique role in Haydn's maturation as a symphonic composer and is, in reality, a Janus-faced composition, pointing simultaneously to the composer's youth and also his future orchestral accomplishments. This observation holds true for a discussion of compositional processes as well. All five species of Fuxian counterpoint appear in this movement; the fugue is finely crafted with a stretto appearing at the point in which the recapitulation would normally appear in a more orthodox sonata form; yet it is precisely this baroque quality that has appeared as a feature of modernity to several generations of scholars with particular reference to the next body of symphonies, those of the <u>Sturm und Drang</u>.

Sturm und Drang Symphonies

Symphony No. 39 in A minor is the first work of the <u>Sturm und Drang</u> period. The first movement displays a slight increase in the number of occurrences of solos, unisons, and periods of silence over that found in previous symphonies; however, these serve as semiotic agents, and the generative force of the movement is provided by sequences, sequences allied with other compositional processes, and imitative writing. In any event, neither the semiotic nor generative processes are unique to the <u>Sturm und Drang</u>; all have appeared quite frequently in the Fürnberg-Morzin symphonies. The remaining movements are distinguished by various disruptions of sequential passages. One pair of disruptions serves as a motto beginning for both movements two and three. Measures 1-3 of the second movement, in which the sequence pattern is disrupted by the viola and cello in measure 3, is closely related to measures 1-3 of the third movement. Obviously, Haydn was continuing his efforts to unify the various movements of his symphonies, a process begun in the Fürnberg-Morzin works. Interestingly enough, in the final movement it is precisely the viola and cello lines that are strict in sequential passages (e.g., measures 48-53 and 56-57), providing compensation or counterbalancing for the disrupted sequence patterns originally encountered in movement two in which the viola and cello lines were the disruptive agents.

The idea of compensation is further advanced in Symphony No. 35 in Bb major although utilizing a different compositional process from its predecessor. In movement one a chromatically ascending bass line is conspicuously present three times (at mm. 27-30, 121-126, and 143-144).[24] No similar process occurs until the fourth movement in which a descending diatonic bass line is presented twice (at mm. 16-20 and 109-113). The internal movements are punctuated almost entirely by solos and unisons.

Symphony No. 59 in A major, while not representative of the concept of compensation, nevertheless reveals its indebtedness in terms of compositional processes to the works of Haydn's early career. Written at the point in time in which the proponents of the traditional interpretation of the Sturm und Drang believe the composer to have become increasingly preoccupied with motivic development, this work displays a greater emphasis upon motivic repetition than development. In fact, measures 95-100 of the first movement contain three successive occurrences of a two-bar phrase in the viola and cello lines. This appears to be representative of the work given

---

[24]The second occurrence of this phenomenon (at mm. 121-126) is a chromatic fourth, a very ancient technique having its origins in the fifteenth century. The irony of its appearance here is that much is made of the early music techniques present in the minor-keyed Sturm und Drang symphonies (e.g., the use of canonic writing and the cantus firmus), while a very old technique such as the chromatic fourth receives scant attention when it appears in a major-keyed symphony.

that imitative writing, in which repetition rather than development is its <u>sine qua non</u>, occurs very prominently in three of the work's four movements (one, three, and four). The fourth movement, a sonata form without development, contains extensive examples of species counterpoint in addition to a wide array of combinations of suspensions and sequences and the aforementioned imitative sections. As was so often the case with the Fürnberg-Morzin symphonies, the simple formal-complex process theorem once again appears to be affirmed.[25]

The reverse of the simple formal/complex process theorem, namely, that movements with complex harmonic structures tend to be generated by a few (generally simple) compositional processes is affirmed by the next <u>Sturm und Drang</u> symphony, No. 38 in C major. Similar to the C major symphonies of the Fürnberg-Morzin group (such as No. 33), the development section of the first movement of Symphony No. 38 touches upon a number of tonal levels (V, v, ii, I, vi, and IV) while the movement is generated almost entirely by long sections of syncopation articulated by short unison passages. In addition, the second movement of this work is characterized by a type of "hocketing" technique, not unlike what was noticed previously as characteristic

---

[25]The simple formal-complex process theorem is just that--a theorem which appears to be true in many or most cases but cannot be verified with an unerring degree of certitude. Although this theorem is useful in examining the interacting of musical forms and processes, it is not a precise predictor or model of eighteenth-century musical construction, as Haydn was perfectly capable of abandoning long-held inclinations. More appropriately, the simple formal-complex process theorem is an indicator of the generally inverse complexity of form and process and helps to indicate a level of compositional activity that probably was not the object of conscious deliberation on the part of Haydn.

of movement one of Symphony No. 15.

"Hocketing" is also the prominent compositional process of the next work in chronological order, Symphony No. 49 in F minor. Likewise, the remaining movements are each motivated by a single compositional process: movements two and four by sequences, and movement three by suspensions. There is also an approximate equality of complexity of form and compositional processes in all four movements. This consistency is significant because Symphony No. 49 (like the Fürnberg-Morzin Symphony No. 11) is one of the few works of Haydn's symphonic output in which the same basic tonality occurs in all movements of the composition. This suggests not only another similarity between the Fürnberg-Morzin and <u>Sturm und Drang</u> symphonies, but a consistently high degree of awareness on the composer's part of tonality as a determinant of both aesthetic and structural function.

The following symphony, No. 58 in F major, can be cited as further support for the simple formal-complex process theorem. The first movement's development section contains only one tonal level (vi) besides the dominant, yet the range of compositional processes is extremely wide, entailing three instances of a disrupted sequence pattern in the viola and cello lines, suspensions, sequences with suspensions, and several types of paired imitation (especially at mm. 42-50 and 129-133). Similar to what has already been demonstrated above in Symphony No. 39, the first and third movements of Symphony No. 58 are unified by a motto beginning, which is, in fact, a disrupted sequence. The motto appears in measures 1-3 of movement one, while a permutation of the motto appears in the initial three measures of movement three. This permutation is reiterated almost immediately (mm. 13-15) as if to draw the listener's attention to this deceptively simple unifying agent. The fourth movement is a sonata form without development, but unexpectedly the composer does not utilize a wide variety of processes; rather, he chooses to use only regularly spaced sequences to provide the forward impulse of the movement. Haydn, therefore, was flexible enough in his use of compositional devices to avoid redundancy and the cliché.

Symphony No. 26 in D minor forms, along with Symphony No. 58, another pair of similarly constructed symphonies. Like its predecessor, the first movement of Symphony No. 26 has a tonally simplistic development, but with a very wide variety of compositional processes present, ranging from syncopation, sequence, and unison to excellent examples of species counterpoint. (See Symphony No. 26, movement one, mm. 17-41 for a fine example of species counterpoint with a long-note cantus firmus in the oboes.) The relationship between the Symphony No. 26/Symphony No. 58 compositional pair is further strengthened by the fact that the former is pitched in the relative minor (D minor) of the latter (F major), leading credence to the suggestion that tonality, rather than modality, is the prime determinant of both aesthetic and constructive function.

Another compositional pair is formed by the following <u>Sturm und Drang</u> symphonies, Nos. 41 and 48, both pitched in C major. In formal terms, the two symphonies display marked similarities, with no movement in either work having a development with more than two tonal levels besides the dominant. Symphony No. 48 is distinguished by a wide variety of compositional processes; the variety of compositional processes in Symphony No. 41, however, appears to be quite singular by individual movement, but when taken as a whole, forms a very unified chain of steadily increasing complexity. The first movement of Symphony No. 41 features two presentations of a tonal sequence (the first of which occurring at mm. 27-38). Although the musical goal of the process is reached at measure 34 (G major), the sequence continues on in its tonal form. Haydn was limited in his selection of sequential patterns because the musical goal was reached very rapidly. There would not have been enough time for a figurative sequence; likewise, an abortive sequence would have negated the feeling of closure at measure 34. In movement two the only distinguishing compositional process is a tonal sequence at measures 44-48. Finally, in movement four only figurative sequences appear, such as that occurring at measures 38-44, one of four such occurrences. The unfolding of the symphony, therefore, is clearly motivated by the gradual fulfillment of the idea of the sequence from the tonal to the figurative variety.

Symphony No. 44 in E minor, the next <u>Sturm und Drang</u> symphony in chronological order, stands by itself in this chapter, forming no compositional pair with another work. This symphony is very consistent, with a similarity of formal construction in all four movements, none of which has a development with more than two tonal levels in addition to the mediant or dominant. Keeping true to form, Haydn allies these four movements of relatively simple formal outline with a large variety of compositional processes. The simple formal/complex process theorem is given corroboration in a number of disparate circumstances, from the naive minuet of movement two with its rather sophisticated <u>canon in diapason</u> to the sonata form of the final movement which features, among many other compositional processes, the presentation and fulfillment of an abortive sequence. This abortive sequence occurs at the outset of the movement, a position that Haydn has favored in the past for the presentation of other disrupted sequential passages (e.g.,

Symphonies Nos. 39:2, 39:3, 58:1, and 58:3). (See Symphony No. 44, movement four, mm. 1-4.) After its initial statement, the fulfillment of the abortive sequence occurs in short order. (See Symphony No. 44, movement four, mm. 19-26.)

A compositional pair is formed by the next two symphonies, Nos. 52 in C minor and 43 in Eb major. Both works are concerned primarily with unisons, solos, and periods of silence as compositional processes. The similarity of the two symphonies is significant because the former symphony is pitched in the relative minor of the latter symphony. This type of relationship between two works of related tonalities is similar to that already seen in the compositional pair of Symphonies 58 and 26, and suggests a unity of design in Haydn's compositional thinking, seeking, as it were, a consistency of process and form in paired works rather than motivic and/or thematic unity.

Symphony No. 42 in D major is not a component of a compositional pair in terms of process. As seen earlier in this chapter and in Chapter II, it was very typical of Haydn to have followed most compositional pairs with a work of greatly different design. Haydn's fascination with various types of sequence patterns is the most remarkable feature of Symphony No. 42, especially in the first and fourth movements where abortive, tonal, and figurative sequences are the predominant processes. The composer is very consistent in distinguishing among the three types of sequences by employing a different syntax for each type. In this symphony abortive sequences always appear immediately before a tonal or figurative sequence; they never appear in a solitary manner but always as an antecedent phrase requiring completion. As an example, the abortive sequence at measures 9-12 of the fourth movement is followed by a figurative sequence at measures 13-14. Figurative and tonal sequences, however, do, appear as freestanding entities, and the idea of the sequence reaches its final fulfillment at measures 141-142 of movement four in which the figurative sequence from measures 13-14 now appears without its accompanying abortive sequence from measures 9-12.

The next symphony of the Sturm und Drang period, No. 51 in Bb major, displays little of the complexity of compositional processes seen in its predecessor. The second and third movements concentrate on one process each (solos and sequences respectively), again demonstrating Haydn's ability to motivate an entire short movement by using only one process or even a single occurrence of one process. The fourth movement is a rondo, like the fourth movement of Symphony No. 42, but in this case the lone abortive sequence is entirely freestanding. (See Symphony No. 51, movement four, mm. 73-76.)

Symphony No. 45 in F# minor ("Abschied") is hardly able to be perceived as revolutionary in terms of compositional processes, adhering as it does to the basic tenets of Haydn's compositional procedures and to the more specific matters of the idiosyncratic presentation of particular compositional processes. The first movement, although pitched in a singularly unusual tonality (F# minor), nevertheless is not at all that adventurous, containing a development that ventures only to the levels of IV, IIb, and VI in addition to the mediant and tonic. The relative lack of complexity of the formal structure, however, is simultaneously linked with a wide variety of compositional processes (syncopation, suspension, and periods of silence) which change very rapidly throughout the course of the movement and prove the movement's very sharply defined forward thrust. The second movement is most notable for the descending chromatic fourth in the bass line which occurs at measures 166-176. Even though this is a relatively unusual feature in an eighteenth-century symphony it has already appeared in Symphony No. 35, movement one and is, therefore, not a unique feature of this work which is considered by so many to be the epitome of the <u>Sturm und Drang</u>. The minuet and trio of movement three is motivated solely by several occurrences of suspension, once again showing Haydn's preference for employing only one specific type of compositional process in a short movement. Finally, the fourth movement exhibits an abortive sequence (at measures 61-64) that is resolved figuratively in the opposite direction within a short space of time (at measures 82-87). The fulfillment of the abortive sequence is most certainly within the practice of Haydn dating back to the Fürnberg-Morzin Symphony No. 27, movement one. Taken out of their chronological contexts, many of the processes employed in Symphony No. 45 would appear unusual; however, when considered in the framework of Haydn's entire career as a symphonic composer these same processes appear to be part of an established routine.

Symphony No. 46 in B major is similar in formal complexity to its predecessor with a slight decrease in the range and rapidity of change of compositional processes. No abortive sequences are seen and, like Symphony No. 45, very little imitation is in evidence. Although most of the proponents of the traditional interpretation of the musical <u>Sturm und Drang</u> specify a preoccupation with baroque contrapuntal practices as a component of the style, it is somewhat ironic that, with the exception of such overt instances as the <u>canon in diapason</u> minuet of Symphony No. 42, imitation does not play an important role in the compositional processes of most <u>Sturm und Drang</u> symphonies; in fact, unisons, solos, and homophonic writing appear to be the most representative of the compositional processes of the <u>Sturm und Drang</u>. The irony is further compounded due to the fact that the compositional processes of the <u>Sturm und Drang</u> which appear to be unique to the style (e.g., syncopation, periods of silence, and those few ostentatious examples of imitative writing) are, in reality, the remnants of Haydn's earliest period of compositional activity. The "unique" features of the <u>Sturm und Drang</u>, therefore, are those compositional processes which are of a rather mundane nature.

Symphony No. 47 in G major is just such a work of the <u>Sturm und Drang</u> era in which the appearance of uniqueness of compositional process is belied by the mundanity of the bulk of its musical material. The specific reference is to the third movement minuet and trio <u>al roverso</u> where both sections are repeated in the retrograde. In spite of its unusual nature Haydn does not use retrograde movement in conjunction with any other type of compositional process besides species counterpoint and homophony. Haydn again presents his compositional processes with an ironic twist: the species counterpoint and homophony is, in reality, representative of the <u>Sturm und Drang</u> while the retrograde minuet and trio is atypical of the era. Movement four of this work is a fascinating compendium of practices rooted in the composer's past and also those which will be seen later in his London symphonies. One example of an established compositional process is the use of an abortive sequence that is almost immediately fulfilled by a figurative sequence. (See Symphony No. 47, movement four, mm. 147-154 abortive sequence, mm. 157-164 figurative sequence.) The movement also points to future techniques such as the repetition of processes and themes seen in the later symphonies of Haydn in which the lengths of the individual movements are greatly increased. One interesting example of a tautological presentation of a compositional process is seen in movement four in which a four-bar bass pattern is repeated three times, then twice (at a different tonal level), then presented once, and finally repeated three times. (See Symphony No. 47, movement four, mm. 75-86, 139-146, 191-194, and 237-248.) The importance of this early appearance of conspicuous tautological processes is that it is another instance of Haydn anticipating or trying out musical techniques that will be employed regularly at a later date. As seen earlier in this chapter and in Chapter II, what seem to be neologisms of style and process in Haydn's music are almost invariably techniques that were developed and tested at an earlier time.

The final symphony of the Sturm und Drang era, No. 65 in A major, a short and seemingly ingenuous work when compared to Symphonies Nos. 45, 46, and 47, is more complex than would appear at a first glance. The formal designs of all four movements are very simple, yet there is a wide variety and number of compositional processes employed throughout the work, especially movement two. The simplicity of Symphony No. 65 is also belied by a great deal of thematic unity among movements two, three, and four. The solo, reiterated pedal in the first violin part of measures 8-16 of movement two is later repeated in the same movement in a contrapuntal context (at measures 81-91). The trio of movement three features two related passages of reiterated notes in the first violin (at measures 33-35 and 45-46), while the fourth movement features two different measures of unison, reiterated notes that serve as important harbingers of syntactical change (first at measure 26, then at measure 69). Symphony No. 65, therefore, like the Fürnberg-Morzin Symphony No. 3, stands as the representative of present and past musical styles and also as the indicator of the future direction of Haydn's creative impulse.

London Symphonies

A cursory examination of the London symphonies immediately reveals several specific ways in which this group of symphonies differs from both the Sturm und Drang and Fürnberg-Morzin groups. To begin with, unisons, solos, and periods of silence begin to occur more often in the London symphonies than has been seen previously. Also, these three compositional processes are less likely to function as signs of syntactical change. Secondly, with only a few notable exceptions, compositional processes in the London symphonies appear in a more autonomous manner than has been seen previously. This is a very logical phenomenon because due to the increased lengths of these symphonies there was no need for Haydn to group his processes together; in fact, the singular appearance of individual processes was almost a necessity given the greater length of performance time with which the composer was dealing. Finally, repetition of compositional processes and motives/unaltered (i.e., unaltered, but appearing in different syntaxes) assumes a greater role in the London symphonies than before; due, no doubt, also to the increased lengths of the works themselves. None of these features, however, are exclusively characteristic of the London period; rather, they are the final working out of stylistic idiosyncrasies that have their origins in Haydn's earlier periods of symphonic composition.

The first London work, Symphony No. 96 in D major, demonstrates the increasing importance of the tautological presentation of musical ideas. In movement three, a unison theme appearing at measure 40 is immediately repeated twice as part of a contrapuntal texture. (See Symphony No. 96, movement three, mm. 40-45.) In movement four the idea of the abortive sequence and its resolution (in the opposite direction) is present. Although this is a technique used by Haydn in both the Fürnberg-Morzin and Sturm und Drang symphonies, in this movement the composer adds a new dimension, making the abortive sequence appear and resolve twice. The first instance of the abortive sequence is at measures 9-11 and resolves at measures 121-124. The second appearance of the abortive sequence appears at measures 158-161 and resolves at measures 219-222.

The following symphony, No. 95 in C minor, merits our attention because it is the only London symphony pitched in a minor key, and, as such, it is a useful model for comparison with the minor-keyed Sturm und Drang symphonies. In terms of formal outlines, Symphony No. 95 is roughly comparable in terms of harmonic complexity when compared to the minor-keyed Sturm und Drang symphonies. The first movement of Symphony No. 95 has a development section that goes into the submediant and subtonic tonal levels which is approximately as adventurous harmonically as the minor-keyed Sturm und Drang symphonies. The development section of the fourth movement (measures 32-105) is presented in a fugal manner. This and other examples of baroque counterpoint in the London symphonies belie the claim made by many scholars that an emphasis on the contrapuntal procedures of the baroque is a determining characteristic of the Sturm und Drang symphonies. As we have already seen, such contrapuntal practices are common to each of the three periods of symphonic composition with which this book is concerned.

The increase in the employment of unison passages is especially evident in Symphony No. 93 in D major, particularly movement three in which the only motivating force besides 1st, 2nd, and 3rd species counterpoint is the unison. The fourth movement, a sonata rondo, possesses a very simple formal outline but utilizes an extremely varied range of compositional processes. One process combination is noteworthy, being a simultaneous presentation of a sequence pattern, a chain of suspensions, and imitative writing between the first violin and cello. (See Symphony No. 93, movement four, mm. 139-145.) The above example is one of the few (and most complex) occurrences of process combination in the London symphonies. As has been remarked earlier in this chapter, due to the increased lengths of the movements, Haydn generally utilized his compositional processes in an autonomous manner in the London symphonies.

Symphony No. 94 in G major displays further the idea of the reiteration of thematic material in changing compositional processes. An interesting example of this is seen in movement one where the unison passage at measures 101-105 becomes a solo passage at measures 106-107 in the first violin. Here Haydn is using thematic material to go from a more complex process to a simpler one. As already seen in Symphony No. 96, movement three, the composer at times could proceed from the simple to the complex (particularly the unison at measure 40 reiterated twice at measures 41-44 in a contrapuntal texture). Flexibility in the deployment of compositional processes (even to the point where orchestration becomes a significant compositional process in itself) seems to be of paramount importance in these late symphonies; no longer are processes rigidly associated with particular semiotic functions. The second movement, from which the symphony derives the appellation "Surprise," is motivated by the variations technique --a technique that becomes increasingly important in this final stage of Haydn's artistic career. Ironically, it is the theme and variations technique that most aptly indicates the composer's overriding concern with compositional processes rather than motivic or thematic development because, by definition, the theme and variations requires thematic stability vis-à-vis a constantly changing context of compositional processes. The only factor unifying the theme and variations is the theme itself which must remain relatively stable instead of being radically altered as it passes from one compositional process to the next. Any notion that the London symphonies contain more thematic development than the Fürnberg-Morzin or <u>Sturm und Drang</u> groups cannot be reconciled with the types of macrocosmic compositional processes that Haydn was employing at this late period. The lengths to which Haydn went in preserving the theme in a more or less pristine state is seen in Symphony No. 94, movement two, measures 83-106 in which the melody is performed simultaneously with a countermelody. The use of the countermelody will also be seen later in different contexts from that of the variations. Haydn also displays extreme subtlety in fulfilling abortive sequences. As an example, in movement four, the abortive sequence occurring at measures 44-46 is finally fulfilled at measures 161-162, but only in the viola and cello/bass lines.

  Haydn also continues to compose similarly structured symphonies in pairs. One such instance is the following pair of symphonies, No. 98 in Bb major and No. 97 in C major. Both symphonies are motivated primarily by solos, unisons, and periods of silence. In Symphony No. 98, for instance, the entire fourth movement is based on the use of solos, unisons, and periods of silence with the lone exception of a sequence occurring at measures 148-160. In the past, Haydn would have used a single sequence pattern or chain of suspensions to provide the forward thrust of a single movement. In Symphony No. 98, movement four, on the other hand, the lone sequence pattern serves to relieve the tedium brought on by a long succession of similar compositional processes. Symphony No. 97 is constructed in a like manner, with only the third movement employing compositional processes (specifically sequences) not frequently observed in the other movements of the work.

Baroque practices once again play an important role, this time in Symphony No. 99 in Eb major. Imitation and fourth species counterpoint are employed quite frequently in this work, but no more so than in measures 128-149 of movement four which even contains a section of stretto imitation (at measures 128-134). The interior movements, however, are motivated mainly by unisons, solos, and periods of silence.

Symphony No. 100 in G major presents some interesting evidence that the seemingly ingenuous quality of the London symphonies masks a high degree of subtle complexity and sophistication. The overall plan of compositional processes in movement is just such a case in point. The movement's exposition and recapitulation are both given forward impetus by sequence patterns, whereas the development section makes use of unisons. This is a very distinct shift in the usage of unisons from Haydn's Fürnberg-Morzin and <u>Sturm und Drang</u> symphonies in which unisons generally appeared in the exposition and recapitulation. The result of this shift is that Haydn is allowing the development of movement one of Symphony No. 100 to be much more stable than the exposition and recapitulation. This is partly the result of the increasing harmonic complexity of the development sections of the London symphonies which need fewer compositional processes to provide forward momentum. The role of silence as a harbinger of syntactical shift is not as clear-cut as in the previous two groups of symphonies. In movement two the period of silence at measure 81 has its place taken by the tympani solo at measure 122. This is the clearest instance to date of Haydn employing silence as implied music rather than as a rhetorical pause, an extremely sophisticated aesthetic function for what was formerly used as a semiotic device.

The following two symphonies, No. 101 in D major and No. 102 in Bb major, constitute a compositional pair, both concerned to a large degree with baroque compositional practices. The fourth movement of Symphony No. 101 contains a rather lengthy fugato at measures 189-232, while movement one of Symphony No. 102 employs a substantial section of imitative writing at measures 161-182. Movement four of Symphony No. 102 is motivated mainly by sequences, one example of which is a sequence allied with a descending chromatic fourth (at measures 223-228). Imitative writing, fugato, and the chromatic fourth are all compositional processes from the baroque (and even earlier periods of music history), and their presence at such a conspicuous level in the London symphonies clearly demonstrates that they were not determining and/or unique characteristics of the musical <u>Sturm und Drang</u>.

Symphony No. 103 in Eb major is in many ways a compendium of the many types of imitative writing utilized by Haydn in his previous symphonies. In movement one imitative entrances in all four string parts are presented, and then the imitative texture is abated. (See Symphony No. 103, movement one, mm. 94-97.) In movement four imitation with an accompanying countermelody is used in one instance at measures 73-98. The use of a countermelody stems from Symphony No. 94, movement two, but its simultaneous deployment in an imitative setting is highly original. Also in movement four of Symphony No. 103, a four-part imitative setting that is not immediately abated is seen at measures 220-235, as well as imitation between a solo instrument and soli grouping (cello and the other string parts at measures 350-360).

The final London symphony, No. 104 in D major, closely resembles in conception and function the final symphonies of both the Fürnberg-Morzin and Sturm und Drang groups, Nos. 3 and 65 respectively. All three symphonies serve as the summation and synthesis of Haydn's symphonic writing up to the points in time in which they were composed. The unique vantage of Symphony No. 104 is that it is the composer's final thought in the purely symphonic genre and represents a resolution, or at least a coming to terms, of a myriad of compositional processes and devices which the composer had employed steadily throughout his career. Every type of compositional process is employed in this work, with copious examples of all five species of Fuxian counterpoint and a variety of imitative techniques. True to his highly logical and consistent nature, Haydn uses only two tonal levels (vi and II) in addition to the dominant in the development section of the first movement which is motivated by a very wide variety of compositional processes, the final bit of evidence in support of the simple formal/complex process theorem. The final movement is motivated by an abortive sequence at measures 3-4, which is followed by a tonal sequence at measures 38-40, a restatement of the abortive sequence at measures 92-95, and finally the figurative resolution at measures 123-124. he ineluctable resolution of the abortive sequence serves as a fitting metonymy for the seeming inevitability of the procession of compositional processes of a Haydn symphonic movement--an inevitability equally present in the Fürnberg-Morzin, Sturm und Drang, and London symphonies, but one tempered by a highly developed aesthetic awareness and sense of irony.

CHAPTER IV

MORPHOLOGY

> The nature of reason is not to contemplate things as contingent but as necessary.
> -----Spinoza

Introduction

In the previous chapters (especially Chapter III) it has been demonstrated that Haydn seldom began a musical idea that did not reach a point of closure even if the beginning and terminus of the idea were widely separated. At times a musical idea might not even be fulfilled in the same movement in which it began. This observation is valid for macrocosmic entities such as large-scale forms and processes as well as microcosmic details of musical construction. The established harmonic schemes of sonata and rondo forms, and the compensatory functioning of movement-wide plans of compositional processes give the false impression of a great deal of precompositional determinism. Yet a work of music also exists on a smaller level: that of the immediate moment. The themes and motives and the various compositional processes (when not considered in relation to macrocosmic models or plans) of a work of music constitute its morphological apparatus (i.e., the structural devices considered without regard to function). The importance of a morphological analysis of the symphonies with which this book is concerned is that if the same consistency of musical presentation is apparent at a microcosmic level (as has already been demonstrated at the macrocosmic level), and this consistency is demonstrable throughout the Fürnberg-Morzin, Sturm und Drang, and London symphonies, it would tend to refute those who view Haydn's Sturm und Drang symphonies as completely divorced from the mainstream of the composer's symphonic output.

Additionally, a morphological analysis of these symphonies should enable one to perceive a glimpse of Haydn's compositional genius at work at a subconscious level, since morphology, by definition, considers localized structural materials without regarding macrocosmic models. Form and process are archetypal phenomena; the morphological apparatus of a musical composition is at a level in which the composer is least bound by tradition and conscious formulation. This is not to say that a morphological study is an attempt to psychoanalyze the composer; on the contrary, the study of musical morphology is an attempt to apprehend the realization of the implicit goals of localized musical phenomena that may or may not be due to the conscious deliberation of the composer.[1]

Too many musical analytical methods are concerned only with a

---

[1] A true psychoanalytical approach was attempted by Wyzewa in his equating of Haydn's Sturm und Drang period with a supposed bout of lovesickness or grief. Wyzewa, however, only tried to explain the psychological motivation of the composition of the Sturm und Drang symphonies, not the manner in which the symphonies were constructed.

classification of elements according to an <u>a priori</u> system of definitions. A rational explanation of a musical composition is fine to a point; however, just as no one would deny that musical creativity has its unconscious side, so too is the fulfillment of musical phenomena not an entirely conscious act. The results of musical creativity, therefore, cannot be explained by taking into account only the rational decisions made by the composer; one must also take into account the role that intuitive actions play in the composition of a work of music. Speaking about the psychological underpinnings of the composition of music, Alan Walker states:

> Musical analysis is concerned with one question: Why? Each answer poses another group of questions and to veto those which lead on to music's psychological antecedents seems irrational.[2]

The concern with the musical morphology of Haydn's symphonies, therefore, is to answer the "Why?" of the composer's presentation of localized material which was shaped not by ever-present logical plans of musical construction, but by the conscious (and even the unconscious) aspects of creativity.

Fürnberg-Morzin Symphonies

Following the analytical method put forward by Leonard Meyer in his

---

[2]Alan Walker, <u>A Study of Musical Analysis</u> (New York: The Free Press of Glencoe, 1962), p. 127.

highly original article "Process and Morphology in the Music of Mozart,"[3] it is truly remarkable to see the wide range of contexts in these early symphonies in which the noncoincidence of process and morphology is compensated for and eventually realized as though the process has continued unabated. Two musical phenomena seen in the Fürnberg-Morzin group, however, are not usually part of those contexts in which a broken process achieves morphological satisfaction by reaching its tonal goal as though it has proceeded without interruption. The first of these two phenomena is the false reprise which invariably occurs in a context of relative stability and is generally introduced by semiotic agents (such as oblique motion or pedal point), signifying an impending shift in musical syntax. Haydn is conspicuously consistent in not allowing two abortive musical ideas to occur simultaneously (which would happen if a false reprise were allied, for example, with a broken sequential pattern or a broken series of suspensions). The second of these two phenomena is the abortive sequence. It may appear illogical that the abortive sequence, the most overt of all broken compositional processes utilized by Haydn, would not be allied with a compensatory realignment of process and morphology; however, the results of Chapter III seem to indicate that Haydn generally resolved the implicit goal of the abortive sequence not within a morphological context, but at a much greater distance from where the abortive sequence first occurred, even at times not within the same movement. In the Fürnberg-Morzin group only one abortive sequence (in the second movement of Symphony No. 3 at measures 39-42) realizes its tonal

---

[3]Leonard B. Meyer, "Process and Morphology in the Music of Mozart" The Journal of Musicology 1 (1982), pp. 67-94. For an explanation of Meyer's methodology and its application here, see pp. 3-4 of Chapter I of this book.

goal within a morphological context. In the following examples in chapter IV, the original music of Haydn's will be given on lines marked (a); immediately beneath this in lines marked (b) will be given the continuation of the process to the point of process-morphology realignment.

Example 1. Symphony No. 3:2, mm. 39-47: mm. 39-42 abortive sequence; m. 47 tonal goal of abortive sequence.

Example 2. Symphony No. 15:1, mm. 44-47: mm. 44-45 sequence.

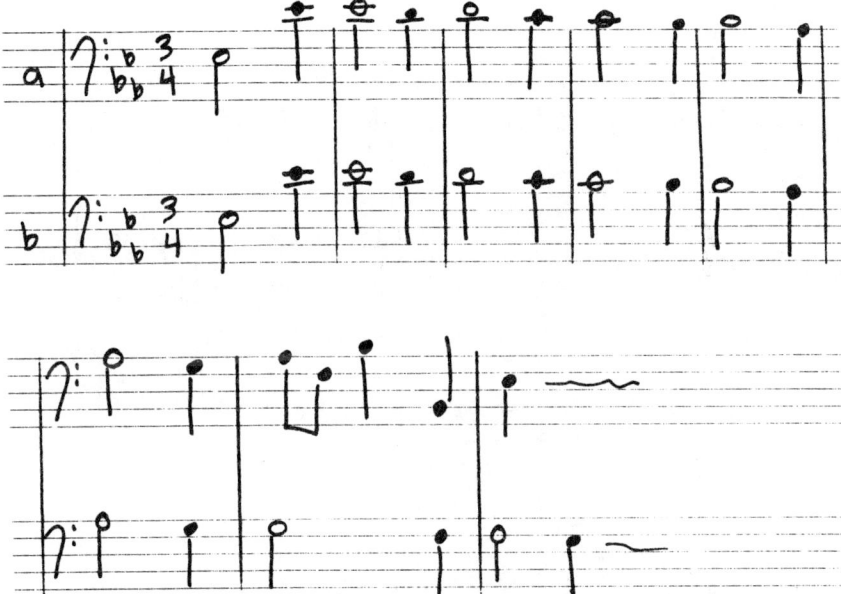

Example 3. Symphony No. 37:2, mm. 35-42: mm. 35-40 figurative sequence.

Example 4. Symphony No. 37:3, mm. 35-43: mm. 35-37 figurative sequence.

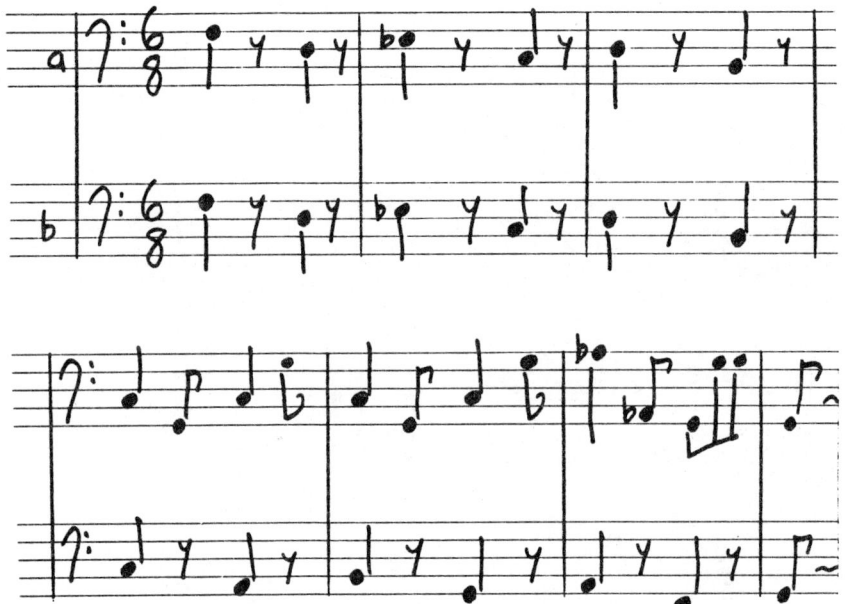

Example 5. Symphony No. 27:2, mm. 25-31: mm. 25-27 figurative sequence.

Example 6. Symphony No. 107:3, mm. 15-18: mm. 15-16 figurative sequence.

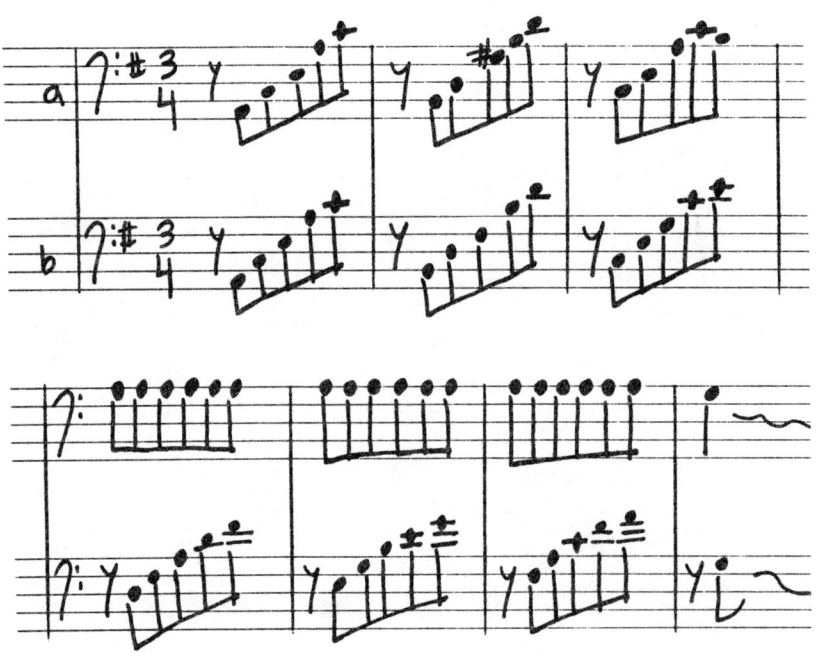

Example 7. Symphony No. 3:1, mm. 66-72: mm. 66-68 figurative sequence.

Sturm und Drang Symphonies

Like their Fürnberg-Morzin counterparts, none of the Sturm und Drang symphonies have false reprises occurring in the midst of, or following, broken compositional processes. False reprises generally follow an agent of syntactical shift (such as unisons, solos, and periods of silence) as was the case with the earlier group of symphonies.

Only two of the abortive sequences found in the Sturm und Drang works are broken off before the completion of the morphological units in which they appear and yet proceed to the tonal goals they would have reached if coordination between process and morphology had not been interrupted in the first place. A typical example of this is seen in the fourth movement of Symphony No. 51:

Example 8. Symphony No. 51:4, mm. 73-80: mm. 73-77 abortive sequence.

One extremely long example of process-morphology realignment occurs in the fourth movement of Symphony No. 45 in which the implicit tonal goal of the abortive sequence elides with a subsequent figurative sequence:

Example 9. Symphony No. 45:4, mm. 61-87: mm. 61-64 abortive sequence; m. 81 tonal goal of abortive sequence; mm. 81-87 figurative sequence.

The underlying regularity of the morphological construction of this movement (which is not readily apparent at a first listening or analysis) is such that seemingly an unknown or subconscious force is guiding the very short abortive sequence to its point of tonal realization and morphological conclusion seventeen measures after it had been broken off. Whether this logical progression of musical events is a product of the conscious or intuitive aspects of Haydn's creative mind (or both) is really beside the point. What is abundantly clear, however, is that this orderly framework belies the image of the "Farewell" Symphony (and by extension, the rest of the <u>Sturm und Drang</u> symphonies) as irrational in conception and construction.

Haydn occasionally allows his compositional processes to extend beyond the tonal goal of the morphological unit. In Example 10 below, the figurative sequence reaches its tonal goal at measure 117, but then is overcompensated for by the extension to measure 120:

Example 10. Symphony No. 41:1, mm. 111-120.

135

Examples 11-18 below are instances of sequential patterns (seven figurative and one tonal) in the <u>Sturm und Drang</u> symphonies in which process and morphology achieve coordination after the sequence has been broken.

Example 11. Symphony No. 38:1, mm. 100-110: mm. 100-105 figurative sequence.

136

Example 12. Symphony No. 38:4, mm. 21-36: mm. 21-26 sequence/suspensions provides link to mm. 31-36 sequence/suspensions.

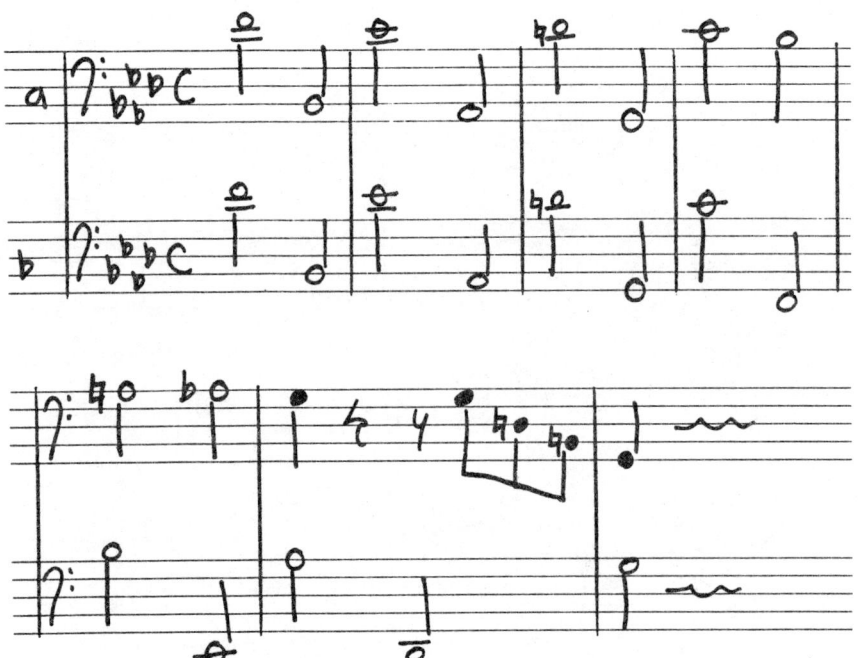

Example 13. Symphony No. 49:2, mm. 65-71: mm. 65-67 figurative sequence.

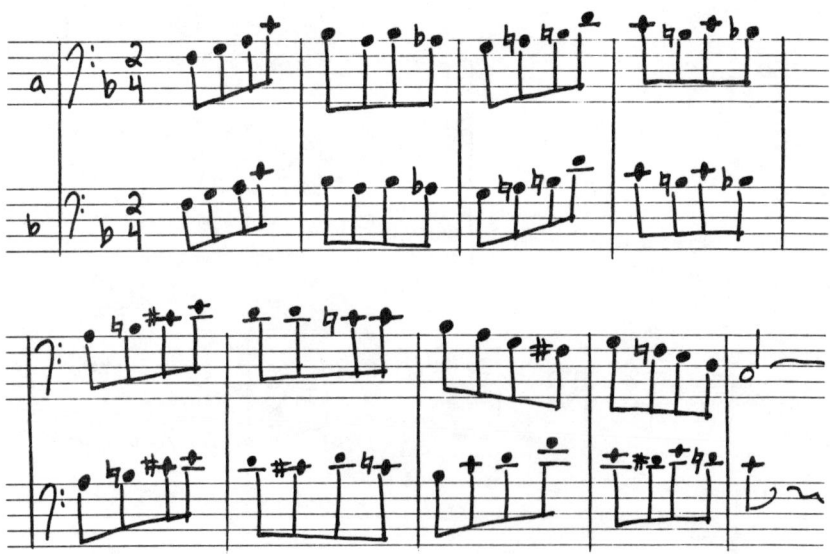

Example 14. Symphony No. 41:2, mm. 44-52: mm. 44-48 tonal sequence; mm. 44-52 tonal sequence (viola & cello/bass).

Example 15. Symphony No. 48:2, mm. 25-29: mm. 25-27 figurative sequence.

Example 16. Symphony No. 48:2, mm. 76-80: mm. 76-78 figurative sequence.

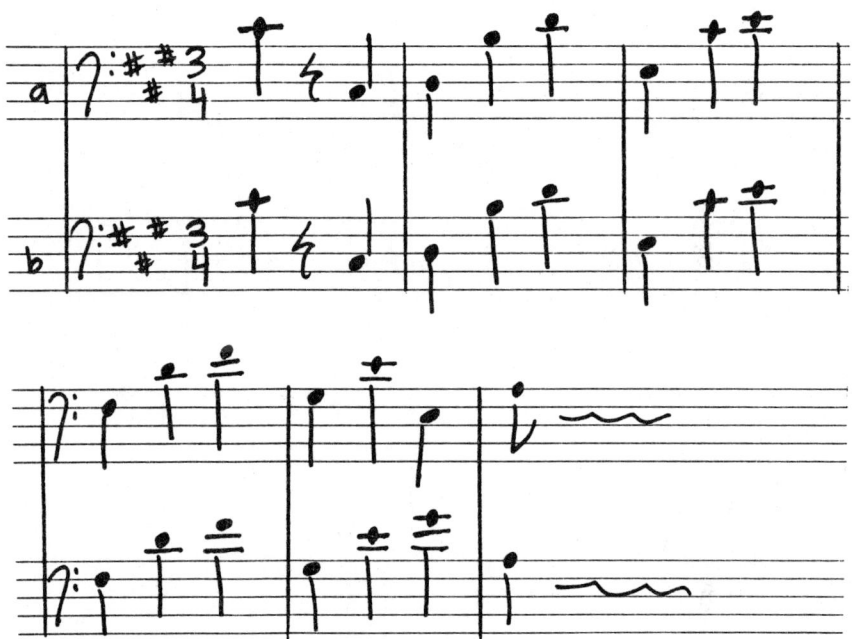

Example 17. Symphony No. 45:1, mm. 33-38: mm. 33-37 figurative sequence.

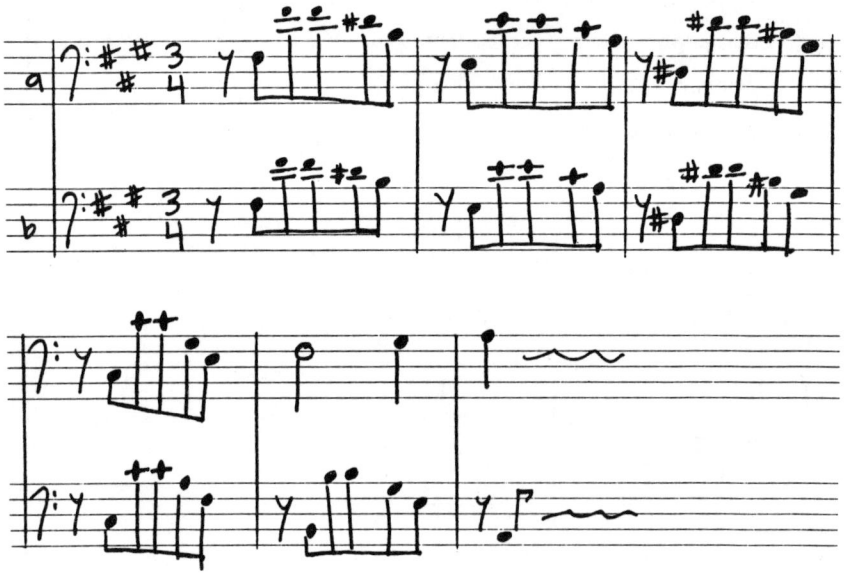

Example 18. Symphony No. 45:1, mm. 50-55: mm. 50-53 figurative sequence.

London Symphonies

As was already noted for the Fürnberg-Morzin and Sturm und Drang symphonies, in the London symphonies there are no instances in which the noncoincidence of process and morphology is allied with either false reprises or abortive sequences and is compensated for and eventually realized as though the process has continued unabated.[4]

Four samples of sequence patterns (three figurative and one tonal), in which a similar realignment of disrupted compositional processes and morphology is realized, occur in the London symphonies.

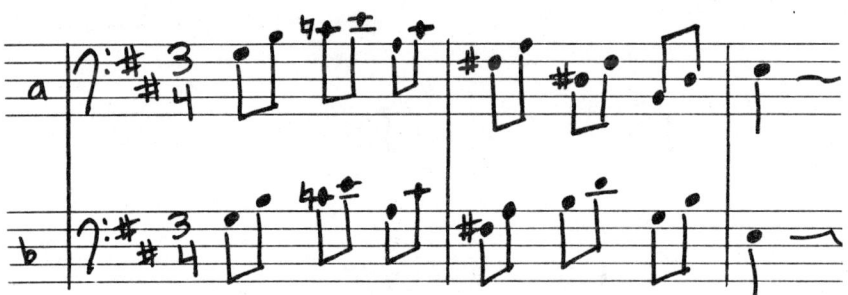

Example 19. Symphony No. 96:1, mm. 139-141: mm. 139-140 figurative sequence.

---

[4]The false reprise occurring in Symphony No. 97, movement one, m. 143, however, is unusual in that it emerges as the tonal goal of a figurative sequence and does not follow a harbinger of syntactical shift such as a solo, unison, or oblique motion.

144

Example 20. Symphony No. 95:4, mm. 137-144: mm. 137-143 figurative sequence.

145

Example 21. Symphony No. 94:4, mm. 161-164: mm. 161-162 figurative sequence.

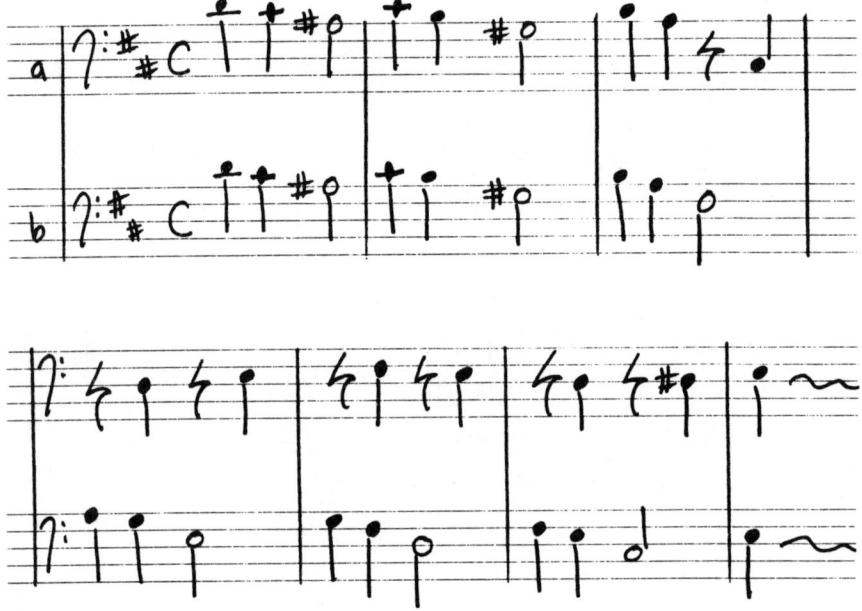

Example 22. Symphony No. 104:4, mm. 38-44: mm. 38-40 tonal sequence.

In review, it is apparent that process-morphology coordination is approximately equal in the Fürnberg-Morzin, <u>Sturm und Drang</u>, and London symphonies in relative terms. Additionally, process-morphology coordination seems to transcend any rigid alignment with a particular type of formal pattern, occurring in both movements of simple formal design and those of a complex formal structure. Haydn is also very consistent in all three groups of symphonies in keeping the compensatory functioning of process-morphology coordination from an alignment with other disruptive phenomena, particularly false reprises. The role of the abortive sequence vis-à-vis the realignment of process and morphology is also dealt with in a consistent manner with only three examples of this present in the forty four symphonies discussed in this book. It would seem logical to surmise that abortive sequences would contain the bulk of process-morphology coordination since the abortive sequence, by definition, is a disruptive compositional process. Ironically, this is not true, and the vast majority of abortive sequences find their implicit tonal goals realized outside the morphological units in which they appear. This phenomenon is again consistent in all three groups of symphonies.

Most telling, however, is the observation that process-morphology coordination is a prominent feature of several important <u>Sturm und Drang</u> symphonies. This coordination is the seemingly subconscious realignment of a disrupted compositional process with its implied tonal goal within a morphological unit as though the disruption had not occurred. That a work such as Symphony No. 45, considered by many to be the most unique and eccentric symphonic composition of Haydn's career, should share the same underlying compulsion to fulfill its implicit musical goals on a microcosmic level as the earliest and last symphonies of the same composer, suggests that the so-called musical <u>Sturm und Drang</u> does not represent an unrelated and autonomous stylistic phase, but a continuity of musical thought at a subconscious, as well as conscious, level.

CHAPTER V

CONCLUSIONS

> We shall not cease from exploration
> And the end of all our exploring
> Will be to arrive where we started
> And know the place for the first time.
> -----T. S. Eliot, "Little Gidding from Four Quartets

As has been discussed in this study, Haydn's symphonic output of ca. 1767-1772 has been traditionally interpreted as resulting from a period of emotional and/or mental pathos which was linked with the German literary Sturm und Drang. The so-called Sturm und Drang symphonies of Haydn, however, preceded the literary movement and yet the sobriquet has remained the chief means by which to identify the symphonies and other works of Haydn's middle period of compositional activity.

Aside from the discrepancies in time between the musical and literary movements, one of the most troubling features of the stylistic designation of

Sturm und Drang is that musicologists have never agreed upon the musical characteristics to be subsumed in this category. In Chapter I, the theories of the leading proponents of the post-Wyzewan interpretation of the musical Sturm und Drang were examined, and it was revealed that the only point in which there was universal agreement was in regard to the preponderance of material in the minor mode. Yet even the minor mode is not a convincing distinctive feature of the musical Sturm und Drang because it is not unique to the ca. 1767-1772 time period, nor do all the Sturm und Drang symphonies (even some of those written in the minor mode) employ large sections pitched in minor keys. In fact, as revealed in Chapter II, some of the most advanced Sturm und Drang symphonies in terms of formal construction are pitched in rather mundane tonalities, such as C major.

The notion that the Sturm und Drang symphonies of Haydn are more given over to developmental procedures than their earlier and later counterparts does not hold up under close scrutiny. It was noted in Chapter II that sonata form movements in the Sturm und Drang symphonies have development sections that on the average constitute 26% of the total musical material of the movements in which they are contained. In the London symphonies this figure is 27% and, contrary to established thinking, in the Fürnberg-Morzin works this figure is 29%. Obviously, there is a great deal of consistency throughout Haydn's entire symphonic production; however, this is contrary to the traditional interpretation of the musical Sturm und Drang.

Consistency of design is apparent in almost every facet of Haydn's orchestral writing. This consistency in no way imparts a chilling sameness upon the composer's works; rather, ex pede Herculem, each particular musical phenomenon gives the listener an inference of the all-consuming greatness of each work as a whole, and by extension, to the entire corpus of Haydn's symphonies. Haydn uses tonalities in a very consistent and logical manner. Works in ordinary tonalities generally have complex formal structures, while unusual tonalities are generally allied with relatively simple formal schema. Likewise, the simple formal-complex process idea, seen in Chapter III, appears in a uniform manner in the Fürnberg-Morzin, <u>Sturm und Drang</u>, and London symphonies.

Furthermore, consistency extends not only to the overt manifestations of Haydn's formal outlines and processes, but also to their underlying, implicit musical goals. In the discussion of musical morphology in Chapter IV, it was demonstrated that in all three groups of symphonies the musical goals of disrupted compositional processes almost invariably reached their goals as though the processes themselves had gone on unabated. This suggests that Haydn's approach to composition was not only teleological in nature, but that Haydn's symphonies are <u>Gestalts</u> in which an alteration at any point in the composition will of necessity impinge upon the entire structure of the work.

This book, therefore, presents a different picture of Haydn's <u>Sturm und Drang</u> symphonies than seen heretofore, and hopefully the comparison of these works to the symphonies of the Fürnberg-Morzin and London groups will begin a process whereby these symphonies of Haydn are better understood within the entire body of the composer's symphonies. Although this first step is a modest one, several ideas concerning those symphonies which were not the central focus of this book (namely, the Fürnberg-Morzin and London works) begin to emerge. First of all, the Fürnberg-Morzin symphonies, appearing at first glance to be rather simple in design, are really quite densely concentrated works, and certainly their complexity tends to belie their early date of composition. Secondly, the London symphonies are not the throwbacks to a simpler and gentler galant style of composition, nor are they the aggressively advanced compositions of the composer's later years. Rather, the distinguishing characteristic of the London symphonies is their increased length over their earlier counterparts. As observed in Chapter II and III, however, length is not a determining factor of musical complexity; instead, the length of a composition directly affects the length of time between the important events of a musical form: the greater the length of a composition or movement, generally, the greater the length between events.

In a more general sense, another observation that may be derived from this study is that since the evidence strongly goes against the idea of sudden and radical stylistic development in the case of Haydn's Sturm und Drang symphonies, an hypothesis may be advanced to the effect that stylistic development is not given to sudden changes of a profound nature. On the other hand, given the overwhelming consistency of approach in Haydn's oeuvre, it is just as unlikely that stylistic development is a slow evolutionary process, at least in the space of a single composer's lifetime. In Haydn's case, from this study it appears that the basic elements of the composer's style were present at the beginning of his artistic career, and were utilized throughout his entire creative life. In this sense, past discussions of stylistic development have considered style evolution as a fait accompli and have arranged the individual musical phenomena in such a way as to support the idea of a progressive metamorphosis of musical styles.

Finally, although this study was limited to determining by comparative analysis the suitability of an intellectual concept surrounding a small group of symphonies by one composer, there are hopefully a few points that may be of some benefit to other musicological endeavors. The most perplexing issue regarding Haydn's Sturm und Drang symphonies is not Wyzewa's original use of the term (which is forgivable given the lack of accurate information in 1909 concerning the dating of Haydn's symphonies), but how later scholars, who had the benefits of improved scholarship, could allow such a rupture to remain between the hypothetical (and often brilliant) suppositions of intellectual/cultural historical criticism and the improved information made available by musical philologists and theoreticians. The answer to this must lie, therefore, with the traditions and processes of musicological research itself. As Carl Dahlhaus had remarked:

> Although scholars vying for membership in the musicological guild exercise excruciating care in ferreting out and hoarding individual facts or series of facts, they are nevertheless allowed to utter vague platitudes when defining collective concepts such as 'neo-romanticism' or 'late romanticism' without tarnishing their reputations as they would by getting their numbers wrong or by connecting absurdly contradictory facts.[1]

A rapprochement is in due order in musicological studies between positivistic and critical methodologies. Only when all parameters and contexts of a musical composition or groups of compositions are considered does true musical understanding begin to occur, and it is only in this manner that future music historical problems such as the Sturm und Drang issue can hope to be resolved before they are irremediably ingrained into the core of musicological thought. But it is undoubtedly too late to hope to efface the idea of a musical Sturm und Drang. Although the term Sturm und Drang is highly

---

[1] Dahlhaus, Foundations, p. 137.

inappropriate for use as a style designation of eighteenth-century music, it would be naive for musicologists to think that the term can be expunged from the jargon of musical discourse, especially after more than seventy five years of use. The term has entered the nebulous world of music appreciation texts and popular culture. A recent issue of TV Guide implores its readers to view a special program devoted to Judy Garland whose vocal style, we are told, is a manifestation of "the Sturm und Drang of Miss Garland's personal life"; in his novel The Burn, the Russian author Vassily Aksyonov refers to the period in Soviet history known as the "Thaw" as "our little Sturm und Drang period"; in a recent issue of USA Today the actor Ed Asner says that "he'd forgotten the Sturm und Drang" of appearing on a regular television series; and one of the regular columnists of New York magazine says of comedienne Tracey Ullman, "when the routine demands, she [Ullman] can sing up a Sturm und Drang." In fact, the term Sturm und Drang has become for fashionable book and record reviewers a substitute for the overused word Angst. The best that can be hoped for, therefore, is that educated people will come to the realization that the term Sturm und Drang in a musical context should be taken with more than a grain of salt.

BIBLIOGRAPHY

Blume, Friedrich. Classic and Romantic Music. New York: W.W. Norton, 1970.

Brook, Barry S. "Sturm und Drang and the Romantic Period in Music." Studies in Romanticism 9 (1970): 269-284.

Dahlhaus, Carl. Foundations of Music History. Translated by J. B. Robinson. Cambridge: Cambridge University Press, 1983.

Geiringer, Karl. Haydn: A Creative Life in Music. 3rd ed. Berkeley: University of California Press, 1982.

Gresham, Carolyn D. "Stylistic Features of Haydn's Symphonies from 1768 to 1772." In Haydn Studies. Edited by Jens Peter Larsen, Howard Serwer, and James Webster. New York: W.W. Norton, 1981, pp. 431-434.

Grim, William E. "Form, Process and Morphology in the Sturm und Drang Symphonies of Franz Joseph Haydn." Ph.D. dissertation, Kent State University, 1985.

_____. "A New Look at the Sturm und Drang: A Comparative Analysis of Haydn's Symphonies Nos. 2, 45 ('Farewell'), and 73 ('La Chasse'). Paper presented at the Fall Meeting of the Southeast Chapter of the American Musicological Society, Virginia Polytechnic Institute, Blacksburg, Virginia, October 1, 1983.

Joseph Haydns Werke. Cologne: Joseph Haydn-Institut and Munich-Duisburg: G. Henle Verlag.

Kolk, Joel. "Sturm und Drang and Haydn's Operas." In Haydn Studies. Edited by Jens Peter Larsen, Howard Serwer, and James Webster. New York: W.W. Norton, 1981: 440-445.

Landon, H. C. Robbins. "La crise romantique dans la musique autrichienne vers 1770." In Les influences étrangères dans l'oeuvre de W. A. Mozart. Edited by Andre Verchaly. Paris: Recherche Scientifique, 1958, pp. 27-41.

_____, ed. Critical Edition of the Complete Symphonies of Joseph Haydn. Vienna: Universal Edition.

Landon, H.C. Robbins. Haydn: Chronicle and Works. 5 vols. Bloomington: Indiana University Press, 1976-1980.

Lang, Paul Henry. Music in Western Civilization. New York: W. W. Norton, 1941.

Larsen, Jens Peter. The New Grove Haydn. New York: W.W. Norton, 1983.

_____. "Some Observations on the Development of Viennese Classical Music." Studia Musicologica 9 (1967): 115-139.

LaRue, Jan. "Multistage Variance: Haydn's Legacy to Beethoven." The Journal of Musicology 1 (1982): 265-274.

Levarie, Sigmund and Levy, Ernst. Musical Morphology: A Discourse and a Dictionary. Kent, Ohio: Kent State University Press, 1983.

Levy, Janet M. "Texture as a Sign in Classic Music." The Journal of the American Musicological Society 35 (1982): 482-531.

Mann, Alfred. "Haydn's Elementarbuch: A Document of Classic Counterpoint Instruction." Music Forum 3: 197-237.

_____. The Study of Counterpoint from Johann Joseph Fux's "Gradus as Parnassum". Revised ed. New York: W.W. Norton, 1971.

Meyer, Leonard B. "Process and Morphology in the Music of Mozart." The

Journal of Musicology 1 (1982): 67-94.

Ratner, Leonard G. Classic Music: Expression, Form and Style. New York: Schirmer Books, 1980.

Reti, Rudolph. The Thematic Process in Music. New York: The Macmillan Co., 1951.

Rosen, Charles. The Classical Style: Haydn, Mozart and Beethoven. New York: W.W. Norton, 1971.

_____. Sonata Forms. New York: W.W. Norton, 1980.

Rudolf, Max. "Storm and Stress in Music, Part II." Bach: The Quarterly Journal of the Riemenschneider Bach Institute 3 (1972): 3-6.

Salop, Arnold. "Intensity in the Classical Sonnata-Allegro." In Studies on the History of Musical Style. Detroit: Wayne State University Press, 1971, pp. 215-250.

Schenker, Heinrich. Harmony. Edited and annotated by Oswald Jonas. Translated by Elisabeth Mann Borgese. Chicago: The University of Chicago Press, 1954.

Sheldon, David A. "The Galant Style Revisited and Re-evaluated." Acta Musicologica 47 (1975): 240-270.

Steblin, Rita. A History of Key Characteristics in the Eighteenth and Early Nineteenth Centuries. Ann Arbor: UMI Research Press, 1983.

Treitler, Leo. "Structural and Critical Analysis." In Musicology in the 1980s: Methods, Goals and Opportunities. Edited by D. Kern Holoman and Claude V. Palisca. New York: Da Capo Press, 1982, pp. 67-77.

Walker, Alan. A Study of Musical Analysis. New York: The Free Press of Glencoe, 1962.

Westrup, Jack A. "The Paradox of Eighteenth-Century Music." In Studies in Musicology. Edited by James W. Pruett. Chapel Hill: University of

North Carolina Press, 1968, pp. 118-132.

Wyzewa, Theodore de. "A propos du centenaire de la mort de Joseph Haydn." Revue des deux mondes 51 (May-June 1909): 935-946.

Index of Haydn Symphonies Discussed in Text

1: pp. ix, 38-39, 65, 89-90, 92
2: pp. ix, 25, 41, 42, 44, 51, 54, 57, 61, 65, 90, 94-95, 98
3: pp. ix, 44-45, 66, 91, 101, 112, 125, 131
4: pp. ix, 27, 42, 65-66, 71, 90, 97
5: pp. ix, 23, 43, 65, 91, 98, 99fn23
10: pp. ix, 25, 42-43, 47, 65, 91, 97-98
11: pp. ix, 23, 43-44, 47, 51, 61, 66, 71, 91, 98-99
15: pp. ix, 41-42, 51, 54, 65, 90, 95-96, 105, 126
18: pp. ix, 23, 40-41, 71, 93-94, 99fn23
21: p. 23
22: p. 23
26 ("Lamentatione"): pp. viii, 22, 30, 49, 66, 106, 108
27: pp. ix, 44, 66, 91, 100-101, 129
28: p. 26
30: p. 23
32: pp. ix, 43, 65, 72, 91, 98
33: pp. ix, 44, 45, 51, 54, 61, 66, 71, 91, 100
34: p. 23
35: pp. viii, 47-48, 66, 91, 103
36: p. 26
37: pp. ix, 39-40, 51, 61, 65, 71, 90, 93, 127, 128
38: pp. viii, 48, 51, 53, 66, 71, 91, 104-105, 135, 136
39: pp. viii, 26, 46-47, 66, 75, 91, 102-103, 105, 108
41: pp. viii, 49, 51, 53, 61, 66, 72, 91, 106-107, 134, 138
42: pp. viii, 50, 52-53, 58, 61, 67, 72, 91, 108-109, 110
43: pp. viii, 27, 50-51, 61, 67, 72, 91, 108
44 ("Trauer"): pp. viii, 7, 9fn6, 23, 25, 27, 31, 50, 66, 107-108
45 ("Abschied"): pp. viii, 7, 9fn6, 16, 22, 23, 24, 27, 28, 31, 41, 53-54, 62, 67, 74, 91,95fn22, 109-110, 133, 141, 142, 147
46: pp. viii, 54-55, 56, 58, 61, 67, 72, 91, 110111
47: pp. viii, 55-7, 58, 67, 91, 111-112
48: pp. ix, 49-50, 56, 66, 106-107, 139, 140

49 ("La Passione"): pp. viii, 7, 9fn6, 23, 27, 30, 48,
    66, 99fn23, 105, 137
51: pp. viii, 50, 52-53, 61, 67, 72, 91, 109, 132
52: pp. viii, 50, 67, 91, 108
54: p. 25
58: pp. viii, 48-49, 66, 91, 105-106, 108
59: pp. viii, 48, 66, 91, 103-104
65: pp. viii, 55-57, 67, 91, 112-113
73: p. 95fn22
93: pp. ix, 59, 67, 91, 115
94: pp. ix, 16, 59, 67, 72, 91, 115-116, 145
95: pp. ix, 58, 67, 114, 144
96: pp. ix, 57, 58, 67, 91, 114, 143
97: pp. ix, 60, 61-62, 67, 72, 116-117, 143fn4
98: pp. ix, 58, 59fn6, 60, 67, 92, 116-117
99: pp. ix, 26, 58, 62, 67, 92, 117
100: pp. ix, 26, 62-63, 67, 92, 117-118
101: pp. ix, 59fn6, 62-63, 67, 74-75, 118
102: pp. ix, 63, 67, 118
103: pp. ix, 63-64, 67, 92, 118-119
104: pp. ix, 27, 58, 59fn6, 63-64, 67, 92, 119-120, 146
107 ("A"): pp. ix, 44, 66, 101, 130

STUDIES IN THE HISTORY
AND INTERPRETATION OF MUSIC

1. Hugo Meynell, **The Art of Handel's Operas**
2. Dale Jorgenson, **Moritz Hauptmann of Leipzig**
3. Nancy van Deusen (ed.), **The Harp and The Soul: Essays in Medieval Music**
4. James L. Taggert, **Franz Joseph Haydn's Keyboard Sonatas: An Untapped Gold Mine**
5. William E. Grim, **The Faust Legend in Music and Literature**
6. Richard L. LaCroix, **Augustine on Music: An Interdisciplinary Collection of Essays**
7. Clifford Taylor, **Musical Idea and the Design Aesthetic in Contemporary Music: A Text for Discerning Appraisal of Musical Thought in Western Culture**
8. Mary Gilbertson, **The Metaphysics of Alliteration in** *Pearl*
9. Stephen Barnes, **Muzak--The Hidden Messages in Music: A Social Psychology of Culture**
10. Felix-Eberhard von Cube, **The Book of the Musical Artwork: An Interpretation of the Musical Theories of Heinrich Schenker,** David Neumeyer, George Boyd and Scott Harris (trans.)
11. Robert Luoma, **Music, Mode, and Words in Orlando Di Lasso's Last Works**
12. John A. Kimmey Jr., **A Critique of Musicology: Clarifying the Scope, Limits, and Purposes of Musicology**
13. Kent Holliday, **Reproducing Pianos Past and Present**
14. Gloria Shafer, **Origins of the Children's Song Cycle as a Genre with Four Case Studies and an Original Song Cycle**
15. Bertil van Boer, **Dramatic Cohesion in the Music of Joseph Martin Kraus: From Sacred Music to Symphonic Form**
16. William O. Cord, The Teutonic Mythology of Richard Wagner's *The Ring of The Nibelung,* Volume One: *Nine Dramatic Properties*
17. William O. Cord, The Teutonic Mythology of Richard Wagner's *The Ring of The Nibelung,* Volume Two: *The Family of Gods*
18. William O. Cord, The Teutonic Mythology of Richard Wagner's *The Ring of The Nibelung,* Volume Three: *The Natural and Supernatural Worlds*
19. Victorien Sardou, *LA TOSCA* (The Drama Behind the Opera), W. Laird Kleine-Ahlbrandt (trans.)

20. Herbert W. Richardson (ed.), **New Studies in Richard Wagner's** *The Ring of The Nibelung*
21. Catherine Dower, **Yella Pessl, First Lady of the Harpsichord**
22. Margaret Sheppach, **Dramatic Parallels in the Operas of Michael Tippet**
23. William E. Grim, **Haydn's** *"Sturm Und Drang"* **Symphonies: Form and Meaning**
24. Klemens Diez, **Constanze, Formerly Widow of Mozart: Her Unwritten Memoir Based on Historical Documents,** Joseph Malloy (trans.)
25. Harold E. Fiske, **Music and Mind: Philosophical Essays on the Cognition and Meaning of Music**
26. Anne Trenkamp and John G. Suess, **Studies in the Schoenbergian Movement in Vienna and the United States:** *Essays in Honor of Marcel Dick*
27. Harvey Stokes, **A Selected Annotated Bibliography on Italian Composers**
28. Julia Muller, **Words and Music in Henry Purcell's First Semi-Opera,** *Dioclesian:* **An Approach to Early Music through Early Theatre**